THE RELIGIOUS POTENTIAL OF THE CHILD

Experiencing Scripture and Liturgy with Young Children

Sofia Cavalletti

Translated by
Patricia M. Coulter
and
Julie M. Coulter

Catechesis of the Good Shepherd Publications

The original Italian edition of *Il Potenziale Religioso del Bambino,* © 1979 by Citta Nuova Editrice della PAMOM Roma. English translation © 1983 by The Missionary Society of St. Paul the Apostle in the State of New York. This second English edition is published by Liturgy Training Publications with the permission of these copyright holders.

This edition of *The Religious Potential of the Child,* with new Acknowledgment, Foreword, Preface and Index of Presentations, has been prepared by the Association of the Catechesis of the Good Shepherd, Box 218, Mt. Ranier MD 20712; Barbara Schmich Searle, editor.

Nihil Obstat
Jeanette Lucinio, SP
Censor Deputatus

Imprimatur
Most Reverend John R. Gorman, PhD
Vicar General   June 24, 1992

The *Nihil Obstat* and *Imprimatur* are official declarations that a book is free of doctrinal and moral error. No implication is contained therein that those who have granted the *Nihil Obstat* and *Imprimatur* agree with the content, opinions or statements expressed.

Cover design by Mary Bowers
Printed in the United States of America.

18   17   16   15   14   8   9   10   11   12

               Library of Congress Cataloging-in-Publication Data
Cavalletti, Sofia.
      [Potenziale religioso del bambino. English]
      The religious potential of the child: experiencing scripture and liturgy with young children/Sofia Cavalletti; translated by
Patricia M. Coulter and Julie M. Coulter.
            p. cm.
      Previously published: New York: Paulist Press, ©1983. With new
introd.
      Translation of: II potenziale religioso del bambino.
      Includes bibliographical references.
      ISBN 978-0-929650-67-8
      1. Children—Religious life. 2. Christian education of children.
3. Catholic Church—Education. 4. Catholic Church—Liturgy.
5. Montessori method of education.
I. Title.
[BV4574.C38131992]   91-19804
268' .432—dc20 92-19804   CIP

Contents

Catechesis of the Good Shepherd Publications is an imprint of Liturgy
Training Publications (LTP). Further information about these publications
is available from LTP or from the Catechesis of the Good Shepherd,
PO Box 1084, Oak Park IL 60304; 708-524-1210; fax 708-386-8032. Requests
for information about other aspects of the Catechesis should be directed
to this address.

Acknowledgment

When the first Italian edition of this book was published in 1978, the Catechesis of the Good Shepherd was only at its beginnings in America.

The extraordinary development that the Catechesis has had in the United States and in other English- and Spanish-speaking countries in these last 13 years calls forth a renewed and deepened sense of gratitude toward those who faced the difficulties of beginning and toward the many people who have come to participate little by little in this experience. We now see the Catechesis of the Good Shepherd in 29 states, involving several thousand children and hundreds of catechists.

All of this fervent labor in the United States has led to the creation of the Association of the Catechesis of the Good Shepherd. Its goal is to help adults and children live together a shared religious experience, one in which the religious values of childhood are central. Toward this end, the association coordinates the work, organizes various initiatives for adult formation, and supports ongoing projects. It also maintains contact with the Center in the diocese of Rome, founded in 1954, and with numerous other centers abroad.

Our original Roman group feels profoundly linked to this great family in the dedication to the work and in the heartfelt thanks that it unceasingly offers to God.

S.C.
Rome, December 8, 1991

1

Preface

The Religious Potential
of the Church

Although Sofia Cavalletti's book is, as the subtitle indicates, a report on the experience of working with children, it also is a valuable demonstration of the Catholic tradition at work, and it offers significant insight into a number of broader pastoral areas in the life of the Christian community. I want to suggest, then, that this book is worth pondering not only for what it has to say about the catechesis of young children but also for the principles on which that catechesis is built, principles that are equally applicable in the parish as a whole. The reason why it is possible to extrapolate from catechesis to ministry as a whole is that the catechesis, like the larger life of the believing community, is rooted in scripture and tradition and puts itself at the service of personal lives lived with God in community. The most helpful way of introducing this book may be simply to highlight for the reader some of the thematics of the Catechesis of the Good Shepherd that seem to have broader pastoral application.

The Life with God

Though I believe the catechesis developed by Sofia Cavalletti to be an extremely effective form of socialization into the Christian tradition and the Catholic community, that is not its primary objective. Sofia Cavalletti is never distracted by her own agenda from the real goal of the Christian life: to live a life hidden with God

3

in Christ. Too often religious education is so goal-oriented and curriculum-conscious that it loses sight of its mission to minister to the religious life of the child. Adult education likewise easily degenerates into indoctrination or dissolves into vapid "sharing." Even liturgy can be derailed by being used for self-expressive ends or aesthetic displays.

This never happens with Cavalletti. On the other hand, it is important to recognize that she never explores this dimension of the catechesis: She does not discourse at length about the religious experience of children. It is a mystery to be respected. All she will do, as she does in the first chapter, is report on what we might call the "symptoms" of that mystery: the sense of engagement, the quiet joy, the recognition of the truth of biblical or liturgical presentation, and the short, sharp insights offered spontaneously by children that, together with their drawings, represent the fruits of their contemplation of the mystery. That is what the catechesis is about. Is it not what all ministry is about: encounter with the mystery of God?

This primacy of the relationship with God, the life of grace as we sometimes call it, is not elaborated upon. Instead, it governs the way the catechesis works, and it can be seen, perhaps most clearly, in the role the scriptures play in the catechesis.

The Word of God

There is something of a crisis in preaching and religious education today because of the way scholarly study of scripture has largely abandoned the task of expounding the scriptures as word of God and has become locked into a historical model of biblical studies reconstructing Jewish and Christian origins and the world of antiquity. It is, therefore, as refreshing as it is rare to find someone trained as a biblical scholar returning the Bible to the church as the living word of God and thus to be set alongside liturgy and life experience as a place of encounter with God.

Nevertheless, in identifying all three—liturgy, scripture and life—as potential sources of experiencing God, priority is given to scripture. We learn to recognize God, Cavalletti is persuaded, through the Bible, and more particularly through those events that constitute the basis of Christianity: the life, death and resurrection of Jesus. Hers is a catechesis based not on doctrine or experience but on *kerygma*: on the events that *are* the good news for us now. This is, therefore, a fundamental option that differentiates the Catechesis of the Good Shepherd from most other forms of religious education but that also corresponds to the basic mission of the church—to evangelize. This is not a story about what happened then, so much as it is a proclamation of God's enduring love for us now. It is the role of the church to proclaim the gospel as a living word of God addressed to the people of today.

The conviction that God speaks when the scriptures are proclaimed is at work throughout the catechesis. The scriptures are introduced to the children not as Bible stories or texts with a didactic or moralizing function; rather, "God and his word are active in the religious event" of allowing oneself to be confronted by the text. That is why the "atrium" where the catechesis is held is more like a church than a traditional classroom: less a place of instruction than a holy ground where Christ is encountered in word and action. "All catechesis," she says, "is in some way a liturgy of the word, for . . . it is God's word we are proclaiming to the child" (p. 80).

But, in proclaiming the living word, Cavalletti does not overlook the historical and literary character of the text that bears that word. For the text to speak, some familiarity with the historical and geographical context is supposed, so even the youngest children are introduced to the map of the Holy Land and to the model of the city of Jerusalem. Moreover, it is important to distinguish historical narratives from parables and prophecies, allowing each to speak according to its own genre. The same respect for the text is found in her insistence on textual integrity: "The text is alive when it is complete." Quoting biblical lines in isolation is only legitimate, Cavalletti argues, when speaker and hearers are already familiar with the scriptural context, so that the whole text is evoked in a single phrase or line. Without such contextualization, there is a risk of abusing and manipulating the text to our own ends.

Perhaps most important is the realization that Christianity is about the mystery of God *now* and that children (read "the catechumens and faithful") are to be initiated into present religious reality. Biblical texts belong to the memory of the church in whose light present experience is understood. This leads on the one hand to selecting those texts that are most adapted to the children's stage of development and, on the other, to avoiding texts where the story seems to stand on its own and does not easily lead to theological interpretation. This is in line with a tradition of textual presentation that goes back to the beginnings of Christianity and is described by the fourth-century pilgrim Egeria in terms of the bishop offering first a literal and then a spiritual reading of the text. Augustine, in his influential writing *De catechizandis rudibus,* talks of the need to offer first a "narration" of the deeds of God and then an "exhortation" that lays out the love of God for human beings revealed in the narration. One sees how this approach can, indeed *must*, be rooted in historical-critical scholarship especially in her treatment of the infancy narratives (cf. chapter 6).

This focus on the present revelatory power of the scriptural word is also brought home by its ritualization. The scriptures are not just read to the children: They are proclaimed in a ritual context that tells the participants that what is so solemnly presented is a word beyond all other words. First, there is the ritual setting: the reservation of the scriptures on the lectern, the assembly of the children in a circle, the presence of a candle. Then there is the process of proclamation itself: the teacher presents the content of the scriptural text in his or her own words; then the children, prompted by the teacher's questions, reflect on what they have heard; next the candle is lit and the actual biblical text is read slowly and solemnly from the book; and finally, the children contemplate, or ruminate upon, the word they have heard in drawing or working with the materials related to the word. These post-proclamation exercises are the young child's natural entree to contemplation and contemplative prayer. Sometimes the proclamation will give rise to prepared or spontaneous "celebrations" (pp. 111–112) closely modeled on liturgical forms. In either event, the natural culmination of an encounter with the living word of God is prayer: "The presentation of sacred scripture— parables or historical narratives—should never be disunited from prayer, in a structured or unstructured form. The proclamation is complete when it has been received, and, in one form or another, when it has been given a response" (p. 118).

Surely there is something to be learned from this experience about how the word can transcend mere instruction, whether in liturgical preaching or in contexts such as the instruction of catechumens. We need to learn how to present the text, how to prepare ourselves to listen and how to take it to heart. There may well be different ways of doing it in different situations, but the important thing, as Cavalletti says, is that the method should be appropriate to the content. This conviction that the text needs to be handled in such a way as to allow it to speak as word of God while respecting the genre of the text enables Cavalletti to steer a careful path between the excesses of biblical fundamentalism and the aridity of strictly historical approaches to the text.

Finally, I think it worth pointing out Cavalletti's insistence that faith as encounter with the living God must precede any presentation of Christian moral principles. Failure to respect this priority creates a distorted understanding of Christianity, which makes the encounter with God in Christ problematic. For far too many preachers and teachers, giving a "practical application" of a biblical text means finding some moral lesson in it. Cavalletti, on the other hand, shows the necessity of opening up the theological richness of a text and letting the hearers draw their own moral conclusions after encountering God and God's word in action.

Liturgy

The scriptural word finds its necessary completion, Cavalletti says, "in the listening community that lives in justice and builds itself in the eucharist" (p. 79). Here she raises her perspectives from the little community of the children's atrium to the larger community of the parish. She herself describes how she came to develop her present method of introducing children to the two great sacraments of the parish: baptism and eucharist (chapters 4 and 5), but what is of more general interest is her explanation of the principles underlying her liturgical catechesis in chapter 10, perhaps the key chapter of the whole book.

In this chapter on "The Method of Signs," Cavalletti builds on earlier work done with the parables, especially in chapter 3, and one can now see the importance of starting with the parables and of learning to read all biblical texts on both the descriptive and the symbolic levels. Children are thereby immunized against literal interpretations of scripture and naively realistic views of sacramentality, because they learn from the first to go beyond the words to the "Word" and beyond the signifier to the "Signified." In fact, Cavalletti employs a rather sophisticated notion of "sign" drawn from modern linguistics. Contrary to popular usage that identifies "sign" with "signifier," Cavalletti insists that the sign only becomes sign when it succeeds in linking the signifier to the signified in a relationship of signification. In other words, a sign has two poles, the signifier and the signified, and the sign only functions as sign when the one leads to the other.

Obviously, this cannot happen if attention gets focused exclusively on the signifier or if the participant glides over the signifier to clutch at a familiar concept. Rather, it is necessary that the participant come to the signified *through* the signifier, i.e., through the contemplative handing on of "those sensible elements whose meaning is not exhausted in what we see" (p. 160).

Liturgy, Cavalletti suggests, is primarily a visual experience. It can only "work," therefore, for those who are trained to allow their inner eye to be guided by the unfolding rite to that which is represented but cannot itself be seen. What is required is not interpretation of signs but a mode of presenting the sign-signifier in such a way that the participants are enabled to leap from the seen to the unseen, from the concreteness and specificity of the rites and ritual objects to the disclosure of the invisible, which they both represent and hide.

In her chapters on baptism and eucharist, the author describes precisely how this is done with children. Moreover, this aptitude, learned at liturgy, will in turn make it possible for the believer to "read" the world of everyday life as a world of signs: "Through signs we become accustomed not to stop at what our eyes see and our hands touch." The alternative is to see the world as an aggregate of flat, one-dimensional "facts," and to understand scripture and liturgy in the same literal manner. The common tendency to see doctrines and sacraments as simple literal representations of invisible facts is surely a major pastoral problem in the church today. Sadly, it is a tendency fostered as much by the clergy in their preaching and sacramental practices as it is by inadequate forms of religious education. Here again, Cavalletti, without setting out to do so, offers principles whose applicability, though it must begin in childhood, goes far beyond the religious instruction of children to shape the style and ethos of parish celebrations themselves.

Ministry

We have remarked how, in Cavalletti's view, both scripture and liturgy require an initiation into symbolic ways of looking and reading. Who is to conduct such an initiation and how? In the Montessori-inspired pedagogy of the Good Shepherd catechesis, this is the role of the directress, and what Cavalletti has to say about adult-child relations in general and the role of the directress in particular is easily extended to all forms of ministry.

In traditional models of education, the teacher, who knows, stands before the students, who do not know. The teacher instructs them. With the Montessori teacher, and with the Christian minister I would suggest, the relationship is different. As Cavalletti puts it, in the context of her discussion of the word: "The receivers of the kerygma are the child *and* the adult; they are simultaneously announcers and listeners" (p. 49). Two things are to be noted here:

first, the shared submission of ministers and faithful to the self-disclosure of God, in this case in the word; second, the overcoming of a natural relationship of dependency in favor of mutuality. In this case, the "child" is more than just a youth; he or she is a symbol for all the dependent, marginalized and insignificant persons in society. Ministry is not just bringing instruction, grace or comfort to these needy people but siding with them to hear what God is saying. That is why Cavalletti goes on to say, "Listening is a leaning towards others, the opening of ourselves in a receptive attitude toward the reality around us; it is only the capacity to listen that prevents us from revolving around ourselves" (p. 49). That ability to side with the child, with the marginalized, is a necessary precondition for hearing the word we profess to proclaim. A related manifestation of this same mutuality is the prohibition against using baby-talk with children (p. 112). Cavalletti points out that while adults tend to talk down to children and to present God in childish terms, children themselves have a profound sense of the majesty of God, reflected in the language they use to speak of God.

The role of the minister, then, must be self-effacing. Cavalletti puts it in terms of not needing to be in control, and more specifically of not needing to count the fruits of one's labors. What counts is not whether we get the results we want but whether the faithful are able to drink of the living streams. Cavalletti constantly reiterates this theme throughout the book, insisting that the teacher not come between the child and God but stand back to allow such contact to occur. She sums it all up by saying:

> The catechist's only security comes from faith: in God and his creature, in God who speaks to his creatures. It is necessary to relinquish all other forms of security, in the spirit of poverty. Poverty is, I believe, the fundamental virtue of the catechist. (p. 96)

This is not to say that the teacher/minister has nothing to contribute, only to emphasize that the role is one of "mediation": "a service rendered to the child so that he [or she] may enter into relationship with that source which puts him [or her] in peace" (p. 72). In other words, the role of the Christian minister is to draw on the resources of scripture and tradition to help the faithful identify the saving presence of God in their lives by proclaiming or celebrating those texts and gestures that are likely to disclose the divine presence to these people at this time. The question the catechist must always ask is: "What is the face of God the child needs?" One could well imagine preachers and pastoral ministers asking a similar question about those who are marrying, about the dying and the bereaved, about the penitent and the convert, and so on.

This implies the listening mentioned above. It also implies the preparation of suitable physical and psychological environments where the imagination can flourish and the life of God can be encountered, received and assimilated. As Cavalletti puts it, the role of the minister is to create the conditions under which the teacher may yield to the Inner Teacher. Like the child, all the faithful hunger not for doctrine, not for the community, but for the life of God.

Perhaps most importantly, this requires of ministers that their own faith life be deep enough to handle the questions raised by the marginal. These are questions that go to the heart of the matter, as Cavalletti shows, questions that the "adult Christian" is frequently unable to deal with. These are not so much questions of enormous theological sophistication as they are questions arising out of the prayer and experience of the questioner, like "How big is God?" or "Why do we have to die?" As Cavalletti remarks, children have a nose for what is essential and a knack for disconcerting questions. We "adult Christians" on the other hand find it easier to talk about peripheral things like Guardian Angels than about central matters like the paschal mystery. Too many sermons prove the point, choosing to emphasize the trivial and pass over the gospel just proclaimed. Cavalletti, on the other hand, stands in a long line of Christian catechists when she insists:

> It seems to us that the movement of the spirit is from the center to the periphery, from the essential to the secondary, from the global to the particular. (p. 143)

In short, the model of ministry proposed by Cavalletti in her description of the catechist is one that conforms closely to that of the disciple in the gospel: siding with the "little ones," being more concerned to do the works of God than to succeed on one's own terms, seeing oneself as essentially facilitating people's on-going relationship with God, having an eye for what is essential. Conversely, Cavalletti warns against the dangers of intrusive forms of ministry:

> The catechist who does not know when to stop, who does not know how to keep silent, is one who is not conscious of one's

limits and, after all, is lacking in faith, because, on the practical level at least, one is not convinced that it is God and his creative word that are active in the religious event. The help the adult can give the child is only preliminary and peripheral, and one that halts—that must halt—on the threshold of the "place" where God speaks with his creature. (p. 52)

Community

To many postconciliar Catholics, bred on the twin values of participation and community, Sofia Cavalletti's method will appear at first as strangely deficient in the communitarian dimension of the Christian life. She speaks, invariably, of "the child" in the singular and uses the term "community" a dozen times at most in the whole book.

On closer reading, however, one will notice that the community is mentioned at key moments, while the actual way in which the catechesis is practiced in the atrium has an unmistakable communitarian dimension. Not only do children gather together for presentations and proclamations of the word, and lead each other on in reflecting on what has been presented, but there are also many opportunities for shared work, peer counseling and shared prayer.

Still, it remains odd that, in speaking of the major symbols of the Christian dispensation, more is not made of the community itself as a primordial sacrament. I am inclined to think that this is ultimately a matter of focus. As we have seen, the primary focus throughout is on our personal relationship with God: It is this, after all, that constitutes the "religious potential of the child." That focus is maintained through a self-consciously symbolic understanding of word and sacrament, in which the mystery of God, unseen and unheard to human eyes and ears, is glimpsed fleetingly as a dynamic force in our personal lives. The Christian community and its tradition are the essential context of the whole enterprise, which supposes intense, concentrated interaction between teachers and students, and among students themselves, as well as between individuals and their "works." Even the silence and recollection, such characteristic hallmarks of the Good Shepherd catechesis, are a sign less of individual withdrawl than of individual engagement. It is in the doing of it all that the children are initiated into the community dimension of the Christian life, into its traditions, and into the various modes and levels of active participation. Here community is the inescapable reality; all too often in places where there is a lot of talk of community, the talk is a sign of its absence.

In selecting these "themes" for comment, I have made no attempt to describe them exhaustively. After all, the role of an introduction is to introduce, not to anticipate, what the author herself will say. My hope is that these lines may serve to alert a wide readership to the broader pastoral and ministerial implications of this classic of Christian pedagogy.

But, in the ultimate analysis, the Catechesis, like the Christian life itself, is a *praxis*. That is to say, its dynamism derives from the constant movement back and forth between doing and reflecting on doing. It is not just a practice; nor is it the application of a theory. It is rather, as Sofia Cavalletti and Gianna Gobbi have demonstrated for nearly 40 years, an ongoing exploration into living the gospel life. Thus, while I have been content to single out some of the more important themes (as they seem to me) in her work, the reader cannot be content with such theoretical reflection. The success of this book will be assured if its readers feel compelled to seek out an atrium and to observe the children and the adults engaged in a common enterprise of exploration into God.

Mark Searle
University of Notre Dame
Notre Dame, Indiana

Foreword

An American Experience of the Catechesis

One Sunday morning this past spring, as I sat observing an atrium of three- to six-year-olds, four particular moments in Jesus' life and teachings came to me and seemed to offer a framework in which to share some of my experience of God and the children in the Catechesis of the Good Shepherd.

The first moment is perhaps the most obvious choice. It is a moment, among several others recorded in the gospels, when Jesus welcomes and blesses the children. In Matthew 18:1–4, the disciples ask of Jesus, "Who is the greatest in the kingdom of heaven?" Jesus answers first by calling a little child to him and placing the child before them, then by saying, "Unless you change and become like little children you will never enter the kingdom of heaven." What strikes me first is what Jesus did not say. He did not use this opportunity to tell us that we must protect the children (which, of course, we must). Even more pointedly, he did not seize upon the opportunity to commission us to be religious educators! As always, so it seems to me, Jesus carefully chose the moment and the words, and he taught us the most important thing to know in our relationship with the children: that we are to change and become like them.

What is it about us that must change? What does it mean to become like little children? What are little children like? Can we only answer in such generic ways as: They are little, energetic, readily excitable, basically trusting, easy to please? Do those who don't live with them know even this much about them? Do those of us who do live with them know any more? My experience of Jesus, my Montessori training and my formation in the Catechesis of the Good Shepherd (both of which place a great value on observing children), and my 17 years of experience working with young children, all lead me to believe, deeply and strongly, that in calling us to become like little children, Jesus was calling us to something far more serious and involved than merely trying to emulate a few of their easily observed characteristics. I believe he was calling us to a life-long journey of growth and transformation—of continually turning and changing and becoming always more like them, but I believe he was first calling us to look at them. In order to become like them, we must first come to know them. We must first find out who they are and, especially, what their relationship with God is like.

One of the most distinguishing characteristics of the Catechesis of the Good Shepherd is its call to us as adults, whether religious or layperson, single or married, with or without children, to look at and listen to the children and allow them to lead us to God. So, too, one of the greatest strengths of *The Religious Potential of the Child* lies in its testimony to the children who, through their comments and their artwork (as well as their way of working with the materials), give us some precious insights into their relationship with God.

The Catechesis of the Good Shepherd has been described as the meeting of two mysteries: the mystery of God and the mystery of the child. When we use such a word as "mystery" it indicates our attitude of respect and wonder, our recognition that we are standing before something which is at once both knowable and yet beyond our complete comprehension. If we see young children as mystery in somewhat the same way as we see God as mystery, then we will want to know more about them. We will want to go on learning about them, and, yes, in addition to responding to Jesus' exhortation to become like them, some of us will feel called to serve them.

If we begin with this attitude of respect and with a true hunger to know the child, we will look closely, and we will see and hear a great deal. We will become like them by first looking at the things at which they look and by learning to look at the things in the way they look at them (i.e., at a similar pace and with a similar degree of absorption and involvement), and we will open ourselves to a new and deeper level of enjoyment of the things we contemplate with them.

And at what do they look? To what are they drawn? Specifically, what "religious matters" capture their attention and hold their interest and arouse in them a deep level of response? To speak to this question, I go to a second moment in Jesus' life and ministry, a moment when, it seems to me, he is expressing frustration over being surrounded by "learned people" who are somehow still missing the point. This moment is recorded in Matthew (11:25) and in Luke (10:21): "It was then that, filled with joy by the Holy Spirit, Jesus said, 'I bless you, Father, Lord of heaven and of earth, for hiding these things from the learned and the clever and revealing them to mere children.'"

Who does Jesus mean by "mere children"? The Jerusalem Bible notes that he was referring to the disciples, whom he also called "little ones"; but I believe he was also referring to children in the literal sense, in light of the other moments in the gospels when he placed a child in their midst and said that one must receive the kingdom like a child. And what does he mean by "these things" which are hidden to some and revealed to others? Again, the Jerusalem Bible notes that "these things" refers to the mysteries of the kingdom.

Building on the earlier observations of Maria Montessori, Sofia Cavalletti and Gianna Gobbi and their collaborators have found, after over 35 years of experience in observing children in a broad range of cultural settings, that certain themes consistently arouse deep interest and great joy in young children. Sofia has noted that "the children from three to six years of age have demonstrated particular sensitivity to the following points, among others: Jesus Christ, the Good Shepherd, who protects his sheep and calls them by name; Eucharist as the greatest gift of the love of the Father and of the response human beings give to God; Jesus Christ as 'the light of the world' and baptism as the act with which this gift is given." Some of the richest responses we see in the children in the atrium come when they listen to those shortest and yet most powerful parables of the kingdom: the mustard seed, the precious pearl, the hidden treasure. In the Catechesis of the Good Shepherd, "these things" to which Jesus referred are taken to mean the things most essential to our faith, and the "mere children" are understood to mean even (and especially) the youngest ones!

I remember a particular first-atrium-session-of-the-year, when I was still quite "green" as a catechist and, thus, very concerned with my role, very absorbed in saying and doing things "perfectly." My group of about ten three- to six- year-olds had entered and had been shown how to carry their own chair to form a semicircle for the initial gathering. I had greeted each of them personally, of course, and already I had been struck by a certain serious, questioning kind of look in the eyes of a little three-year-old girl named Katherine.

After we were all settled in our chairs I began my carefully prepared introductory talk about our having come to a very special place called "the atrium" and about why we have come here. I was holding their attention so well—except, that is, for Katherine's. She was not spellbound like the others. Although she was sitting very still, her eyes were moving intently around the room. Obviously, she was looking for something. Suddenly she stared into my eyes and interrupted my little speech, asking "Where's God?" I don't remember what I said; I only remember trying to resume my presentation. A second time Katherine interrupted to ask, "Where's Jesus?" and, later, a third time, to ask, "Where's Mary?" It was only much later that I understood that Katherine knew exactly where she had come and why—even without my carefully prepared speech!

A third moment in Jesus' life takes me to the heart of the Catechesis of the Good Shepherd and, therefore, to the heart of the atrium experience. It is a moment when, as in other moments, people must have been asking Jesus again, "But who are you?" This time he answered by saying, "I am the Good Shepherd." He answered with a parable that is central to our work with the children and from which our catechesis takes its name. All of the parable of the Good Shepherd is rich and important for the children, but, for now, I want to focus on one particular verse, the one that includes "I know my sheep and my sheep know me" (John 10:14).

The most important thing that happens in the atrium (or in our lives, for that matter) is that, together with the children, we grow in our knowledge of Jesus, the Christ, the Good Shepherd, and in his love for us, and that we grow always more capable of responding to that love. As catechists of the Good Shepherd, we understand that the kind of knowledge Jesus speaks of in John 10:14 is not a limited, academic kind of knowledge but a total kind of knowledge that is rooted in the heart and that encompasses all of our being (including, of course, our heads). Sofia has pointed out what many of us have witnessed: how totally the young children are involved in a religious experience. I love the prayer, cited in this book, of the little girl who said, "My body is happy." My favorite response of the children over the past ten years, however, has become that of the deep sigh that often follows the presentation of scripture in a moment of the liturgy. My formation in the catechesis has helped me hear these deep sighs and to understand them as prayer. I continue to be amazed at the depth of their reflections and the degree of their absorption when they are at their chosen work, as well as the delight they take in such simple activities of controlled movement as arranging flowers for the prayer table, or setting out the articles used in the eucharist on the miniature altar table, or making processions to celebrate the change of the liturgical season. Their involvement is so full. Their range of response is broad, from quiet to active work, from deep silence to joyful song.

When the young child meets the Good Shepherd, all of the child is there. And after they have listened to Jesus' own words through the solemn reading of scripture, and after they have chosen a material designed to aid their continued meditation, the real "knowing" happens. Then we are privileged to see something of how the relationship grows. How often I have seen children stand the figure of the Good Shepherd outside the sheepfold and then work very carefully to get each sheep close enough to the Shepherd to be touching him or, at other times, suddenly lift him up and sing out, "Alleluia."

The children know that the Good Shepherd gives all the necessities to us: food, water, safe passage. Adults know this too, don't we? But do we know, as the children do, the other benefits of staying close to the Shepherd? Do we know as four-year-old Elizabeth knew, that "he would take the sheep out to see the bright stars at night," or, like three-and-a-half-year-old Daniel that "he would take them to a good hill and let them roll down it"? Are we so sure, as the children are sure, that when we are lost, he would search for us and call our name until he found us? Do we know that his first response, upon finding us, would be to place us on his shoulders or, as four-year-old Andrew added, that "he would give us a big smile" rather than scold us?

As I have observed the children in the atrium over the past 12 years, as I have listened with them to God's word and heard their responses in the meditation that precedes and follows the reading of the scripture, as I have seen the materials they choose and how they work with them, as I have seen their artwork and have sung and prayed with them in communal worship times, I have become sure that there is a primary question in their hearts and minds: "Who are you, Lord?" I do not believe this question arises from confusion or uncertainty. Rather, I believe it is a question like that of the people who gathered around Jesus when he walked on this earth, those people who felt his touch and heard his voice and saw his face, a question that is really saying, "I've seen you; I've heard you; I know you, but I know there is more of you to know. I need and want to know more."

In so many ways the children have shown me that they are capable of deep religious experience, which I believe means a deep relationship with God. They sense God's presence. They understand

and enjoy God's closeness. After several weeks of carefully preparing the chalice with a lot of wine and a few drops of water, four-and-a-half-year-old J. W. offered his newly found wisdom on this liturgical moment which the church calls "the mystery of the mingling of the water and the wine." J. W. sauntered over to his friend who had chosen the preparation of the chalice work that day. He leaned against the shelf where his friend was working, folded his arms in a gesture of manly confidence and said, "You know what that means? It means God and us—we're very close."

The fourth and last moment I've chosen from Jesus' life and teaching is a proclamation: It is what I call the "why" of the good news. The proclamation is in two parts. The first part is found in the parable of the Good Shepherd, when Jesus says, "I have come that they might have life and have it to the full." The second part is found in the parable of the True Vine, the parable which becomes central in our work with older children, when Jesus says, "All this I tell you that my joy may be yours, and your joy may be complete" (John 15:11). For both children and adults, the atrium experience is one of our hearts "resting" in God, and experience of hearing God and of coming to know God better. So, also, it is an experience of "life to the full" and of joy that is "complete."

Two particular moments in my experience with young children now stand side by side in my memory. The contrast of these two moments concretizes and illustrates for me this fullness and joy. The first moment comes from my initial Montessori teaching experience when there was no atrium. A group of five-year-olds and I had just returned from a walk in the woods with an insect of some kind. Back inside the classroom, Ian turned the insect over and discovered its unusual, multicolored underside. He called the other children over and showed them this wonderful phenomenon. I watched their excitement grow. But suddenly it was over. I was struck by a sense of incompleteness for us all in that moment. Something was missing from the experience.

The second moment is from my first year in the atrium, when a small group of three- and four-year-olds and I had listened together to Jesus' words about the kingdom of heaven being like a precious pearl. I had posed the questions, "How do you think the merchant felt when he got that pearl? What do you think he did?" One child said, "He would put it in a special place." Another child answered, "He would tell his friends about it." Three-and-a-half-year-old Annie just continued staring at the pearl in the shell on the merchant's shelf. Suddenly, she threw up her arms and nearly shouted out, "He wouldn't even want to eat dinner!" There was a long silence, and then the children wanted to sing several songs.

There was a great sense of completion in that moment, the sense that a precious gift has been received and responded to. This is what we understand prayer to be in the Catechesis of the Good Shepherd: the receiving of God's gift to us and our response to that gift. And we understand that the first and most precious response is simply the contemplation and enjoyment of the gift, leading to praise of and thanksgiving to the Giver.

Perhaps it is difficult for us to sense the fullness of life in the atrium or to recognize the particular quality of the children's joy if we have not first discovered our own joy in response to God's presence. But the children help us with this. As we listen with them, somehow the voice of the Good Shepherd becomes clearer, and it is easier to hear our own names being called.

May the children be our teachers. May the joy grow always fuller.

Rebekah Rojcewicz
Christian Family Montessori School
Mt. Rainier, Maryland

Introduction

"I bless you, Father..."
Matthew 11:25

The present volume is intended primarily as a document of the child's spiritual and religious capacities. We have tried as far as possible to let the children themselves speak, either through their own words recorded as they were spoken, or through their drawings. This present work is the outcome of an experience of more than twenty-five years of catechesis with children from three to eleven years of age. We will limit ourselves in this first volume to speak of what we have been able to see in children up to the age of six. The only exceptions are a few references in the first chapter, and the chapter on moral formation where we wanted to document the influence of the work done before six years of age on the motivations of behavior in later childhood.

The method we followed was to observe children in specially prepared centers of catechesis, both private and parochial. Once a week the children spend the major part of an afternoon in the center, thereby having the opportunity to carry out freely chosen activities with the aid of materials that were created for the children and gradually improved on the basis of their reactions. In addition to these centers, the work has been developed in several nursery and elementary schools, thus giving us the means to examine our work in a different context where catechesis becomes a more spontaneous part of the children's life.[1]

With rare exceptions, we have avoided systematic questions. Instead, we tried to understand the child's way of thinking in the course of personal conversations and group discussions. It has been particularly indicative to us to see the children request that some specific subjects be repeated many times, and to observe how they used the material. Time and time again we would see that the children were enchanted by the presentation of certain themes and that they made prolonged use of determinate elements of the materials. When this recurred over a long period of time, then we believed that this was an indication that the subject matter and the manner of its presentation corresponded to the interests and needs of the child. And so an ensemble of elements—few and essential—was slowly delineated, which the child showed that he knew, not in an academic way, but as if they were a part of his person, almost as if he had always known them. With the parables, for instance, some were set aside and reserved for an older age group, and we concentrated on those parables that proved to be a constant object of the child's passionate interest.

This experiment, which originated in Rome with children from middle-class backgrounds, developed rather rapidly in other centers including agricultural and industrial areas, in Rome and the environs, as well as in Africa (Chad), Brazil, Mexico, the United States, and Canada, passing therefore through the filter of children from different cultures. Throughout these varied environments, the children's reactions to the themes presented in this book were always the same. It is this that led us to consider that we were not faced with the personal reaction of this or that individual child but rather with a phenomenon concerning *the* child.

In the first two chapters we will speak of the "actors" of catechesis: God, the child, the adult. We have attempted to document the existence of a mysterious bond between God and the child. This bond occasionally manifests itself following some solicitation—even the slightest and most discreet—on the part of the adult, but it subsists in early childhood even in cases of spiritual "malnutrition" and appears to precede any religious instruction whatsoever.

The manifestations of serene and peaceful joy the children display in the meeting with the world of God lead us to maintain that the religious experience responds to a deep "hunger" in the child. The religious experience is fundamentally an experience of love, and for the human person, love is essential to life. Man is not satisfied with merely living, but living as one who is loved and loving. So we ask ourselves whether the child does not find the satisfaction of an existential need when he comes into contact with the religious reality, which will influence the harmonious formation of his personality and the lack of which will negatively affect the child's life. We would like to recall the words of Bultmann, according to whom the religious act tends toward the "completion of being." A hunger such as this is more deeply felt and evident in the child, who is particularly rich in love and in need of love, as if there were a kind of connaturality between the child and God, who is Love.

The present volume does not take into consideration the child under three years of age, since our experiment begins with this age. However, we do recognize the negative limitations of this. The fact is that one witnesses manifestations in children over the age of three, especially of prayer, that cannot arise out of nothing and that make us reflect on the potentiality of the preceding years, which is little or not at all noted. What this potentiality consists of and how it can be helped is, to the author at least, completely unknown.

In chapter 2 we have tried to elucidate the character and limits of the adult's function, which may be defined as that of the "unworthy" servant of the Gospel. The adult is unworthy in that he serves the child's potentiality, which is not his own, and the Word of God, which does not belong to him, and also because the results of our work always exceed the premises. Nonetheless the adult should be a "servant." The adult cannot evade the service necessary for the child and God's Word, keeping in mind that in the presence of the Word of God not only is there no longer neither Greek nor Jew, but, we believe, neither adult nor child. Before the Word of God we are all hearers of a message that God addresses to His people through events and words. Such a message can be grasped only through a choral listening in which the child's voice may have at times stronger and more profound tones than that of the adult.

In this perspective, the center of catechesis is a place in which the community of children and their catechists live their religious experiences together. The center of catechesis is a place for celebrating the Word of God, for listening, praying, and reflecting together, for meditation and work. It is a place where the child is able to do everything at his own rhythm, which is slower than the adult's; this is how the child can prepare himself to participate more consciously in the community life of the adults.

In chapters 3 to 8 we describe our manner of presenting the individual themes, or, better, how we have reached, after so many attempts, our current mode of presentation. We will also indicate and comment on the most frequent reactions we have observed in the children, trying to clarify, however inadequately, the psychological and theological reasons for these reactions.

These descriptive chapters outline the major themes presented to the child: Christ the Good Shepherd, who protects and defends us, with whom "everything is fine" (*si sta bene*), according to the common expression of the children; the Eucharist as the "sacrament of the gift" in which the Father gives us His presence in our life, the dynamic presence that draws forth in us a response; Christ the Light and Baptism as the act through which Christ transmits His light to us, the light of the risen Lord; the Kingdom of God—we could also speak of the mystery of life—as the mysterious and precious presence, within and around us, of the vitalizing force of God that sustains us, leads us forward, and gives growth. These are the elements that give the children complete security and thus respond to a vital need that is experienced especially in early childhood. These are the elements that place the child's relationship with God on a plane of trusting faith. The older child, the adolescent, the adult, will integrate this level on the basis of the different needs of the various ages, so that the face of God will come to be enriched by other aspects: the God who not only gives His love, but whose love is forgiving; the God who offers, in Christ, an ideal of the heroic life; the God who searches for the relationship of a lover.

Furthermore, these themes we have mentioned emphasize the element of enjoyment in the religious experience. Indeed, we believe that early childhood is the time of the serene enjoyment of God, when the response the creature gives to God consists in the very acceptance of the gift in fullness of joy. The time for a different response will come, a response that will even involve the person in effort and struggle. But we must respect the stages of human development.

Then follow three chapters of a more systematic nature. In the first, "Moral Formation," we have remarked how the Christian proclamation—which was given in early childhood without any moral reference but for the sole purpose that the child receive and delight in it—is later reflected in the older child's life on the level of behavior as well. In this it appeared to us that the proclamation has an immediate effect characterized by enjoyment, and another, longer range effect on the level of behavior, so that the ethical life, concretized in actions, unfolds on the basis of realities already loved and enjoyed. We believe this to be a proof of the fact that what is received in early childhood becomes the substance of the child's life.

Chapter 10, "The Method of Signs," highlights the religious character of this method. The Method of Signs is indispensable, it seems to us, when one wants to speak about the transcendent reality, which all our speech can only approximate. The use of a different method, which, rather than speaking through images in allusive tones, adopts an abstract language and claims to define, risks changing the nature of the content one is trying to transmit. The method must be in some way connatural with the content.

Moreover, the method of signs is not only a necessary means of initiation into Christianity, in which Christ is the greatest "sign" of the Father, but it is also an instrument in the formation of faith mentality. It is a means to accustom ourselves not to limit our field of knowledge to the tangible and visible reality. It is a way to learn how to read the "signs" not only in the Bible and in liturgy, but in the world that surrounds us as well.

Finally, in the last chapter, we ask ourselves whether our catechesis may be called anthropological. We have tried to clarify that our catechesis may be so defined, not because it is based on the isolated experience of this or that individual child, but because it is founded on the fundamental structure of the child. That is to say, we have not looked for the anthropological link of the Christian message in this or that individual experience lived by the child, but rather in the exigencies of the child that may be synthesized, as we said earlier, in the need to be loved and to love. Experience (*esperienza*) offers a basis for this message: a field that has already been tilled—and sometimes ruined—by the life one has already lived and that is, in any event, limited. However an exigence (*esigenza*) is like a hunger waiting to be assuaged; it is like a coiled spring ready to burst forth and, as opposed to experience, presents itself as a virgin dynamism (see chapter 11, section "Experience and Exigence"). Faced with a certain exigence within the depths of the child, we have sought to satisfy it with religious nourishment.

Another occurrence that seemed to us to be of particular significance was to observe how the child coalesced the single themes, presented one at a time, into a synthesis that is frequently rich in theological content and in which the Good Shepherd occupies a dominant position. Many drawings reproduced here verify this: The Eucharist is the pasture to which the Shepherd calls His sheep in order to feed them with His love; in Baptism, the lamb is welcomed into the sheepfold and receives the light, becoming a "lamb of light." Prayer is predominantly praise and thanksgiving to the Shepherd, who accepts us "into his beautiful sheepfold." The figure of the Good Shepherd is sometimes placed beside the Bethlehem cave, and the Good Shepherd and paschal candle are illustrated as two interchangeable images; therefore Christmas and Easter are viewed as historical events in the Good Shepherd's life.

The remarkable fact is that such syntheses were the result of the children's own verbal or pictorial expressions before they were clear to the catechists themselves. We had limited ourselves to offering the single themes with the aim of identifying the aspect of God that corresponded to the needs of the younger children and how to present it. This phenomenon of the spontaneous convergence of the individual components of the Christian message toward the figure of the Good Shepherd—a constant phenomenon in groups of children from extremely diversified environments—was always associated with the manifestations of serene peace and the sense of profound satisfaction we mentioned before. So it was that we asked ourselves if the person of the Good Shepherd could not be the figure that fulfilled in a particular way that religious exigence verified in the child.

The religious experience, as we said, coincides with the most essential vital exigence, in that it is an experience of love. The Good Shepherd "gives his life for his sheep," and he came so that "they may have life, and have it abundantly"; the parable announces to us a plentitude of love that coincides with a plentitude of life. The gift of love about which the parable speaks is not an abstraction, nor is it a gift of "things." The Good Shepherd gives himself to his sheep: he gives his concern, his presence, his guidance, consummating this dedication in death, a death that however brought him to the resurrection.

The gift of the Good Shepherd's love, therefore, not only fulfills the deepest of our vital needs but realizes what seems to be the fundamental law of life. At every level of reality, life appears to unfold through successive "deaths," which lead to fuller forms of life. It is a law we see being carried out around us, within nature and within ourselves, in which life develops through the "death" of the child and adolescent we once were so as to reach ever more complete levels. The secret of reality seems to be in this continuous passage from a "less" to a "more," from a death to a resurrection. The secret of reality seems to be the presence of a seed of life hidden at times in elements that are most opposed to it. The sprout of the resurrection is present even in death. The more it diminishes and conceals itself, the more it appears to become powerful and capable of carrying life toward greater fulfillment. The Christian mystery seems to us the symbolic and historical expression of a law that regulates the growth of the entire universe.

The Christian message, far from leading us away from reality, far from building superstructures, is rooted in the most profound depths of the human person and in the whole of reality. It nourishes the most irrepressible hunger of the person and enlightens all that surrounds one. The explanation for that sense of joyful satisfaction the child experiences by coming into contact with the Christian message is found, it seems to us, in this fundamental correspondence of the Christian message with the vital exigencies of the human person, and with reality itself. Naturally the richness of the Good Shepherd parable is grasped only progressively. However, in our estimation, it is important to base catechesis on a few, essential elements that are able to reveal themselves to the child gradually as he grows through adolescence to adulthood, and that are also capable of leading the person toward an ever deeper penetration of reality.

One may wonder how we can speak of catechesis—though the more appropriate term would be "evangelization"—in relation to children under six years of age, and to see it given a certain systematization indicating a specific number of themes as well as a sequence of presentation linked to the liturgical year. Generally, we think that a vague theism cannot subsist, but that religiousness (*religiosità*) necessarily tends to be configured in a determinate religion. To want to stay on a level of religiousness deprived of content would be tantamount, as Santayana stated, to wanting to speak a language without using a spoken tongue. If we intend to talk about God we must use a language, and the language with which we speak of God takes the name of an actual religion. If, then, we enter the Christian sphere, any vagueness is in particular contrast to the incarnational character of Christianity; the transmission of the message is primordial and fundamental since it deals with a religion based on a Person and an event that cannot be known unless they are announced. Christianity cannot be understood from the simple observation of what we see, as is possible in a religion that is naturalistic in character. Marrou speaks of Christianity as a "learned religion." This is true for adults and, in our view, children as well. All modern psychology points out the incredible capacities of early childhood. Could the religious realm be the sole exception to this? During our times, when we speak of children able to read at three years of age, could the child be irremediably "illiterate" only in the area of religion?

Obviously we do not intend to make the child into a budding theologian (meaning theologian in the pejorative sense of the word). What we have asserted in this book may arouse confusion if, when talking of catechesis or evangelization, we have in mind an abstract and systematized type of exposition found in textbooks. We do not give anything of the kind to children. We try to put the child in touch with those "sources" through which God reveals and communicates Himself in living form; namely, the Bible and Liturgy, in balanced proportion. We would like the child, as a result of an increased familiarity with these sources, to share in the renewal that is growing in the Church in our days. We would like the child to find a more clearly defined position in the Christian community, which today places itself in a special stance of listening in the presence of God's Word. We would like the child—as the equal of and together with the adult—to be counted among the number of "listeners."

In such sources we find the necessary elements to initiate the child into the reading of the third source of catechesis: life. See in particular the chapter entitled "Education to Wonder and the Kingdom of God," where it is explained how, through the use of several parables, the child is helped to open his eyes with wonder and enchantment to the miracle of life and the world around him.

We are aware, and not without fear, that we are proposing some things, especially in chapters 4 and 11, that do not correspond to the contemporary trend of catechetics. It is obvious that we do not profess to make any categorical affirmations. Our intention is simply to communicate what we have seen up to the present time, during a rather lengthy experience with children from very different environments, in which the observation of the children has been our principal guide. We believe that our experience is but a drop in the ocean—even though it extends to include the experience of numerous past students and collaborators. Nevertheless, it may have some value in the exploration of the mysterious world of the child and his relationship with God. We ask those persons who may share some of the views set forth here to take them not as a point of arrival, but as a departure point for a deeper and more developed research. For whatever good there may be in these pages, and above all for the work of which they are the expression, we thank God profoundly, Who has willed to place us in the service of His Word through the child, and Who has guided us toward a more essential penetration of it with the child.[2]

NOTES

1. See the description of the religious aspect of life in the "Adele Costa Gnocchi" Children's House in Rome in the laureate thesis by P. Arbeola Algarra, *Una experiencia educativo-religiosa en niños de cero a cinco años.* Rome: Universita Salesiana, 1971.

2. The experience we describe has been conducted on the basis of Montessori principles. As for the application that has been made of them, this represents a development for which the author and her collaborators are responsible.

Chapter One
God and the Child

*".. . because you have revealed these
things to mere children."*
Matthew 11:25

Before beginning any discussion about the religious education of children, we should ask ourselves a basic question: Is it
justifiable to give religious education to children?

Nowadays we are very careful, and with good reason, not to
impose our own personal choices on others. In initiating children
into some form of religious life, are we not perhaps offering them
something that may be most valuable to us, but without which
the child would be just as happy, the absence of which would in
no way affect the child's life or his harmonious development? Or
worse still, are we not perhaps complicating the child's life with
inessential superstructures that weigh him down with a burden
that does not correspond to his needs?

We must search for the answers to these fundamental questions within the child himself. The adult cannot and should not
reply on a theoretical plane. The response should arise only from
an attentive and impartial observation of the child, so that it is
the child himself who tells us if he does or does not want to be
helped to discover God and the transcendent reality. It must be
the child who tells us if the religious experience is or is not constitutive of his personality. An interpersonal relationship is always a mystery; it is more so when it involves a relationship with
God; when the relationship is between God and the child the
mystery is greater still. Nevertheless, it has been possible at
times to penetrate fleetingly the secret of this relationship; some

documents have been collected that attest to a spontaneous religiousness (*religiosita*) in the child.

The Child's Attraction to God

Maria Montessori, in her book *Spontaneous Activity in Education,* records the account of Professor Ghidionescu at the International Congress of Pedagogy in Brussels in 1911.[1] He reported the case of a child who had not received any religious education; one day the child suddenly burst into tears, saying: "Do not scold me, while I was looking at the moon I felt how often I had grieved you, and I understood that I had offended God." In the same work, Montessori adds other examples that she herself witnessed or that were related to her personally. She cites the example of a seven-year-old boy, also deprived of any religious education, who had been told the theory of evolution according to the principles of Lamarck and Darwin. After the explanation the boy asked: "From whom did the first creature come?" "The first," answered his friend, "was formed by chance"; at these words the child laughed aloud and, calling his mother, he said excitedly: "Just listen; what nonsense! Life was formed by chance! That is impossible." When he was asked how life was formed the child responded with conviction: "It is God."

In this example we are dealing with a deduction that is logical in nature. Cases of this type are fairly common; for instance, Gallo has collected numerous examples relating to deaf-mute children.[2] An intellectual fact of this kind can occur, however, only in children from seven years of age onward; it has the advantage of being easily expressed and therefore also easily verified by the adult.

Nonetheless, it interests us to know if, before this intellectual age, there exists a relationship between the child and God that is more deeply rooted than in the intellect alone. Such an investigation requires instruments of verification that are difficult to obtain, since we must concentrate on facts that are totally spontaneous in the child's life, the expression of which may be less explicit and direct than in the cases we cited.

The following example presents similarities with the one reported by Montessori. However, this one involves a three-year-old girl who grew up without the slightest religious influence. The child did not go to nursery school; no one at home, not even her grandmother, who was herself an atheist, had ever spoken of God; the child had never gone to church. One day she questioned her father about the origin of the world: "Where does the world come from?" Her father replied, in a manner consistent with his ideas, with a discourse that was materialistic in nature; then he added: "However, there are those who say that all this comes from a very powerful being, and they call him God." At this point the little girl began to run like a whirlwind around the room in a burst of joy, and exclaimed: "I knew what you told me wasn't true; it is Him, it is Him!"

We ask ourselves if it is possible to speak of a logical process in this instance (at three years of age!), or if this is not the expression of a different relationship of the child with God—a relationship that manifests itself not only in the enunciation of a truth, but also by means of a joy that appears to touch the deepest part of the child. Examples like this lead us to consider that the religiousness of the young child is so strong that, as opposed to what happens during adolescence, it does not let itself be damaged by negative environmental conditions. In this case we would seem to have an exception to what is generally maintained in the field of psychology, that is, that the person is in some way a child of one's environment. Does there exist in the child a mysterious reality of union with God?

Who would believe that a four-year-old child would be capable of metaphysical intuition? Lorenzo (four years old) belonged to a Catholic family, but he had never had any catechetical instruction nor had he received any special care in the religious sense. One day his aunt asked him to do a picture of God. Lorenzo drew on the bottom left-hand side of the page—hence in a secondary position—a human figure with a large head, and then he filled the page with a series of signs in which numbers could be recognized. His aunt asked him the reason for the presence of the numbers, and Lorenzo explained: "Because they are many." Lorenzo had the intuition that God is infinite.

Evidently we are dealing with transient moments, and we wonder what degree of awareness the child himself has of them. This does not prevent them from constituting true facts of life, which sometimes ferment for a long while within the depths of the child's spirit without his being conscious of it. Read, for instance, the experience written by the famous French novelist Julien Green:

In the course of these dim years, I can remember a minute of intense delight, such as I have never experienced since. Should such things be told, or should they be kept secret? There came a moment in this room when, looking up at the windowpane, I saw the dark sky and a few stars shining in it. What words can be used to express what is beyond speech? That minute was perhaps the most important one of my life and I do not know what to say about it. I was alone in the unlighted room and, my eyes raised toward the sky, I had what I can only call an outburst of love. I have loved on this earth, but never as I did during that short time, and I did not know whom I loved. Yet I knew that he was there and that, seeing me, he loved me too. How did the thought dawn on me? I do not know. I was certain that someone was there and talked to me without words. Having said this, I have said everything. Why must I write that no human speech has ever given me what I felt then for a moment just long enough to count up to ten, at a time when I was incapable of putting together a few intelligible words and did not even realize that I existed? Why must I write that I forgot that minute for years, that the stream of days and nights all but wiped it out of my consciousness? If only I had preserved it in times of trial! Why is it given back to me now? What does it mean?[3]

Another similar moment of intense delight is narrated in the unpublished writings of M. C.:

I was standing in front of an open window one summer evening. A little below the windowsill a roof sloped down, behind which still other rooftops descended, so that the window opened out toward a very wide space. On the nearest roof a cricket sang at intervals in the darkness. I distinctly remember the sharp crack, interrupted and then renewed, that the cricket's sound made in the silence of the night. Yet I remember just as well (and, even more, if I recollect myself, I feel once again) that that perception opened me toward a feeling, or better, to a general state of consciousness which, in a graduated way, but with extreme rapidity and extraordinary power, led me from this perception to a kind of immaterial and universal revelation.

First of all I had the feeling of space, or more precisely, I had the sensation that an unlimited vastness was thrown open before me, and for an instant perhaps I was dismayed before that immensity. Yet, just an instant later, all my hesitation disappeared, swept away by an impetus which arose from the depths of my being, and which urged me ahead and led me to go toward that space, almost as if it were opened solely so that I would expand within it. And this was the first moment that I can distinguish in that swift progression which I experienced at that time.

The next moment, which followed in an imperceptible fraction of time, was distinct from the preceding one because I became aware that an irresistible ardour had been enflamed within me in that moment. I was wholly moved; warm, tender, full of fervour; I overflowed with affection. That movement was, more intimately in me, a violent transport of all my affectivity. From tenderness to avidity, that movement was pervaded by all that I later knew under the name of love. That moment remains present to me, in fact, as one in which a powerful seduction inundated me and enveloped me, and to which I reacted by accepting it and, even more, by wanting it. That movement in space, which I had experienced a moment before for the first time consciously, returned to my mind at that point like an embrace, to which I had been opened up passionately from within the depths of myself, toward an unimaginable thing which revealed itself to me.

And then the third moment came with a continuity which, I would say, was more perfect than what I had experienced up to that point, following the change of my consciousness. Of itself, and truly all by itself, that embrace that I was experiencing was transformed in my heart into an absolute plentitude of joy. An astonishing joy, a kind of enthusiasm of joy, invaded me. I was all aflame in the luminosity of a happiness so intense and complete that I was immobilized by that feeling, in a state that remains in my memory as one of perfect satisfaction and absolute union. And that is how my experience of that event of living concluded that evening.

I am certain that my experience unfolded in the way I have said: from an expansion in space, an act of love, and happiness. It unfolded through a rising spiral, ascending in that way, and drew me, but not more than I felt inclined toward and had decided to follow. I do not know exactly how old I was when that event happened in my life; I think I must have been five years old, maybe six, or perhaps four. The event of that evening is, however, the first memory that I have been able to discover in myself. As much as I have tried, I have not found anything in my memory that precedes it. So I think I am able to date that evening as the birth of my consciousness. I can also say that, even if that event seemed strange to me later on and compelled me to reflect and try to understand it, at the time however it passed over me as something very natural. I am convinced that, in that moment of my life, I was oriented forever toward existence, and that the whole life of my consciousness depends upon it. Still, the event of that moment did not upset my childlike state. I continued to live my childhood in a completely normal way. It was certainly wonderful, what I had known, and yet it was as if that wonder had been at that time something altogether natural.

These are documents of a relationship with God that goes beyond the intellectual plane; it is founded on a deep, existential level. The experience just described is remarkable in its complexity, the nature of which is affective, cognitive, and moral: the certitude of a presence, a presence of love that attracts with a great force of "seduction," but not more than the child was "inclined toward and had decided to follow"; therefore a presence that does not impose but appears to await a response.

Linda related an experience that has some similarities with the two passages just quoted. It is an experience she remembers having happened at the beginning of her life—certainly before the age of six. One day she noticed a butterfly in flight and she felt drawn to it; she followed it and suddenly "everything seemed to open up around me." It appeared that she was able to see everything more clearly, and she "felt filled with joy and warmth throughout my whole body" in a way she had never experienced before. The sensation was so strong that the little girl burst into tears of joy, ran to her mother, and said: "Mommy, I know God." Only much later, in thinking over that event, did Linda associate it with love; at the time it was something "very new and different, for which I had no reference points." It was something that the child did not perceive with her mind; what she had said afterward to her mother "was not an explanation, it was an exclamation."

All three examples deal with religious experiences lived in the first years of life, which oriented the lives of those who lived them, and which pose the problem of the existence of the religious fact in the child prior to any promptings that are cultural in character. Another moment of mysterious encounter occurred two years ago in a little girl from a Roman suburb. Monica (six years old) attended the Montessori school in Tuscolano; there the catechist presented the models and articles relating to the altar and then she took the children to church so that they could see the same objects, this time the real ones. After returning to school with the other children, Monica began to work again with the altar models, her back turned to the class. All of a sudden she stopped, turned around and said: "How happy I am today that I went to church! Mommy never takes me to church, she never has time. At last today there is someone who saves me and I feel free." These are words that, either by formulation or content, seem to surpass a child's capacity; yet the catechist, herself amazed, took note of them immediately, reporting them exactly as she heard them.

As well, the words of Francesco (five years old) do not seem to correspond to a child's level: Francesco must have understood that his mother was not a believer, and he asked her: "Whom do you love more, me or God?" The mother naturally replied that she loved him more and the child responded: "I think this is your big mistake." It would be hard to believe that such an expression could be found on the lips of a child, if the mother herself had not repeated it. Also, it has been observed from many sides that there appears to be a difference between the child's natural and supernatural capacities,[4] and that the religious element in children is not proportionate to the external stimuli.[5]

As we said earlier, we are dealing with ephemeral moments, like a flash of light that shines vibrantly and then fades away.

However, they let us glimpse in some way the mysterious reality present within the child; they manifest the child's potentiality and richness, the nature of which we are not successful in defining clearly. The fact that we are dealing with flashes does not invalidate their importance, because it is proper to the child to live at first in a discontinuous way the riches he possesses, which only gradually and through the aid of the environment later become a constant *habitus* in him.[6]

Children's language is often composed of actions and interior attitudes more than words. Such actions and attitudes, when they recur constantly in different children from diverse backgrounds, make us probe the question of their significance. In reference to this, we would like to speak about the impassioned attraction the child has shown when faced with the religious fact, so much so that he will forget or disregard the things supposedly more pleasing to children. Edda, three and a half years old, was not baptized; she really enjoyed the prayer and celebrations that took place in the nursery school she attended. When the time for holidays arrived Edda went to the country, where she discovered that the farmers went to church and she was not at peace until she went with them. Her parents were very moved by this. They were atheists, but they had great respect for their daughter and they themselves took Edda to the priest to be baptized.

Francesco was two years and two months old. As a Christmas present he received the first tricycle of his life; almost at the same time his mother spoke to him of the meaning of Christmas and gave him a manger scene. Francesco took it happily; completely forgetting his tricycle, he wandered around the house carrying the various pieces of the set, showing them again and again to his grandmother so that she would retell the story of Christmas.

Charlotte (three and a half years old) was staying at her aunt's house. When she saw her aunt preparing to leave she asked her where she was going; the aunt replied that she was going to Mass and the child declared: "I am coming too!" And so it continued for days, without the slightest urging on anyone's part. One day another child came to play with Charlotte and she told her aunt that she would not be going to Mass with her. Then a moment later she was back again saying: "Stefano can wait, first I'm coming with you."

Anne Marie van der Meer also noted something interesting

about her young son Pieterke. Before she and her husband con-
verted, they took a trip to Italy with their five-year-old son; later
she reminisced with her husband:

> Weren't you struck by the way Pieterke, who was
> only five years old, followed the services in the churches
> we visited in Italy? Think of the ceremonies in the ca-
> thedral of Siena and in the Roman basilicas: they were
> never too long for him and he did not want to leave. For
> such a restless boy the opposite would have been natural
> and understandable! He thought the celebrations were
> magnificent. I don't think I have ever told you what he
> asked me as soon as we returned to Uccle from our trip
> to Italy: "Mother," he said to me one day, "why don't we
> ever go to church as we did in Italy?"

Still during the time before her conversion, Anne Marie van
der Meer, at her friend's insistence, told her son that they would
pray the Our Father together at night. "The child was strangely
happy at those words," she noticed; ". . . when I forgot the prayer
on the evenings we were giving a reception, Pieterke never failed
to remind me to say the Our Father with him. I recited it every
night. Meanwhile, even though I was praying this way, we were
not believers. But the child was happy."[7]

Another noteworthy example is contained in the letter sent
to a parish priest in Moscow regarding a little girl whose age was
unspecified but who obviously had to have been quite young:

> . . . having rushed into my room and seen the icons, the
> little girl began asking me questions; . . . with eyes wide
> open she fastened her gaze on the faces of Jesus and the
> Mother of God, which she was seeing for the first time in
> her life. Although with effort, I explained to the child,
> who is a young cousin of mine, the meaning of what had
> struck her in a way she could understand. But my wor-
> ries proved to be superfluous. "You know," she said to
> me, "I knew He existed and I have always talked with
> Him before going to sleep; I knew He was everywhere
> and that He sees me when I get into mischief, only some-
> times I was afraid of Him. How can I speak with Him?"

Moved by the child's words, I taught her the sign of the cross, and I experienced an extraordinary feeling watching those small hands making the sign of the cross on her slender little body.... "And now can I kiss Him," she continued to my great surprise, "but not on His face or cheek, not the way I kiss Mommy? Because He is greater than my mother, He is better than my mother. He sees everything and He doesn't scold me. He is better than everyone, and He loves me. Give me the icon please, I want to see it always. I'll put it beside my bed, and the icon of His mother too. Give it to me as a gift!"

When her mother arrived the child said: "Mommy, quick, come here. Kiss Him. He loves you too. At last I've seen His face, but I've known Him for a long time." Before her mother's embarrassed silence the child continued: "Mommy, why don't you say anything? Mommy, tell me about Him; I need to hear about Him." But the icon was taken away from little Irina. Her mother described the child's reaction: "She cries, she asks to hang it above her bed, saying: 'I want to see Him, I need to talk to Him.' "[8]

The child's attraction toward the religious reality also leads him to become involved in conflict, and to overcome negative environmental conditions. How many children from atheistic families the author has seen who thirst to come close to God! Massimo (six years old) was a difficult child. One day it was necessary to tell him: "If you continue to make such a disturbance I will not be able to let you come again"; Massimo's changed facial expression showed how deeply the warning had struck him. From that day he made no further disturbances.

For children who live in atheistic environments, contact with the religious reality represents, quantitatively, an infinitesimal part of their lives. Why does it have such a hold on them? Why, among all the influences in their lives, do those of a religious nature—even if sporadic and limited—find a special responsiveness in children? Often there appears to be a disproportion between what children receive in the area of religion and what they express. The above-mentioned examples refer to children of different ages, belonging to diversified environments, and thus they demonstrate a diffused attraction in the child toward God.

The Joy of the Relationship with God

Once again I would like to emphasize the joy the child displays when helped in this attraction of his. Maria Montessori observed the joyous enthusiasm with which the children responded to her first endeavors during the time of her initial experiment in the religious field in Barcelona in 1915. She stated that "the Church almost seemed to be the end of the education which the method proposed to give," and that the activities the children did in church were "practically repetitions of what they had learned to do in the classroom. . . . Such things, therefore, must appeal to their tender minds as the end of their effort patiently sustained, giving them a pleasing sense of joy and of new dignity."[9]

Arago-Mitjans has also noted the "particular joy" the child shows when praying, and that when the child is involved in religious activities his "whole being vibrates, becomes tranquil, and rejoices."[10]

The Catechetical Center, whose work we will describe in this book, was brought to birth by the stimulus of the children's joy: Enrico (six years old), Paolo (seven years old), and Massimo (six years old) were meeting for the first time with an inexperienced catechist; Paolo did not really want to come because that was his only free day and he would have preferred to stay at home and play peacefully; for the catechist's part, she was totally inexperienced and without any equipment that could have helped the children—she had only the Bible. The catechist opened to the first page of the Bible, read it, and helped the children to enter into the text. Two hours passed by quickly, and when Paolo's mother came to take him home his eyes filled with tears; he did not want to leave. Massimo was willing to give up the music lessons he loved because he wanted to come to catechesis "every day," because "this is more important."

Born under the banner of the children's joy, the Catechetical Center has grown and lives through the children's joy. A similar phenomenon is verified in other centers where the work that is done follows the same method: The children of Colonna (Rome) devised the trick of moving the hands of the clock ahead so that they could go to catechesis earlier. "Why have you come so soon? [Almost two and a half hours had passed.] I was doing so well," protested Lucia; after her mother's explanation she insisted again: "But I was doing so well." Laura (six years old) said: "I'd like to sleep here, even on the floor." A catechist working in the suburbs complained that the children's meetings were not as orderly as she would have liked; in fact, the children were not content to take turns, but they wanted to come to every catechetical class. When the time for the last meeting of the year arrived, the children wanted to stay indefinitely; Rita (nine years old) said: "It's over, but when do we come back?" and, in the following autumn, when she found out it was too difficult for her mother to bring her, she began to cry. Marco Fabio (six years old) put his open hands on the table and asked: "Will you save my place for next year?"[11]

Far from needing to resort to devices to draw the children to catechesis, catechesis becomes its own reward: "If you are good until Christmas, I will bring you back next year" declared the mother of Stefano (eight years old), who found it troublesome to bring him to catechesis; Stefano made such obvious efforts that his mother could not help but keep her promise though it was a sacrifice for her. "If you are not good, you are not going to catechesis on Thursday" the teacher warned Leonardo, a terror (five years old).

One could object that the child is fond of many things and that many things make the child happy, and this is true. However joy has many qualities: There is the joy that results in making the child nervous, and very often the child who was having fun becomes moody and joy ends in tears. This is not the quality of joy the child experiences when drawing near to God: We are dealing with a joy that puts the child in peace, that makes him serene and calm. Giulia (three and a half years old) was a nervously fragile child; she always returned home from nursery school at noon tired and strained. One afternoon a week she went to the Catechetical Center and her catechist was the same directress who cared for her in the morning at school; after two hours of catechesis Giulia went home relaxed, rested, and tranquil. John (eight years old), Elisabeth (six years old), and Alexandra (three and a half years old) spent a few weeks in Rome. They came with their mother to visit the center, but they were not happy to come, preferring to play; two hours later they left, meditative and happy, and did not think to complain of the long walk they had to make home.[12]

Often mothers have observed that their children are silent and recollected within themselves during the trip home after catechesis. Sometimes the children also express in words a deep enchantment, one that opens them out to love: Ottavio (ten years old) said: "I am so happy, I feel a joy inside me"; another boy (eight years old) remarked: "I love everybody."

Following catechesis, prayer, or the Mass there are never agitated reactions—running around, yelling—that would indicate that catechesis had been an effort for the children or that they had been restrained. On the contrary, the children, satisfied and serene, want to extend the experience, continuing to work reflectively, speaking in subdued voices or singing with intense and tranquil joy. It would appear that a deep chord within the children had been touched and they, as though enraptured, continue to listen to its prolonged vibrations in the secret of their hearts. The reactions we have been able to observe in children resemble those of a person who has found his milieu and, once having found it, does not want to leave.

The response the children give to the religious experience is such that it seems to involve them deeply, in total gratification: "My body is happy" said Stefania after praying a long while with her young friends. The facility and spontaneity of the child's religious expression and prayer, which Arago-Mitjans highlights as well,[13] lead us to believe that these arise from the depths of the child's being, as if they were natural to him.

The Child's Mysterious Knowledge

In the religious sphere, it is a fact that children know things no one has told them. An impressive example, recounted earlier, is that of the little girl who recognized God as maker of the world. Listening to her father's explanation, she felt in some sense betrayed by his words without having the ability to defend herself; it was enough for her father to pronounce the word "God" for the girl to realize what she had been searching for and she clasped it with infinite joy. I would like to say here what I have had occasion to speak of elsewhere: Many years ago I was presenting Baptism to a group of children from four to six years of age, and I was unsure whether or not to speak of the meaning of the imposition of the hands, thinking that it was too difficult for children of that age to understand. But in any event I wanted to try: I put a ring in my hand and two or three times I extended my arm, opened my hand, and let the ring fall out, explaining that this is what I would do if I wanted to give them a gift. Then I repeated the gesture without the ring, saying: "At Baptism, the priest makes this gesture over the child; but you do not see anything fall. Then why does he do it?" The children replied in chorus, as if the question were completely superfluous: "Because he is giving us the Holy Spirit." Two theology students were present; I could see they were startled. Where do the children get such knowledge? I do not know how to respond; what is certain is that they knew.

Years later I wanted to speak to the children about the meaning of the invocation of the Holy Spirit during the Eucharist. Once again I showed them the gesture of the imposition of the hands, and then I sat down and asked: "Why does the priest do this at Mass over the bread and wine?" Without hesitation, Lucia (four and a half years old) answered: "He is calling the Holy Spirit into the bread and wine." Giovanni (two and a half years old) was at the supper table with his parents and, without any connection with the previous conversation, he suddenly said: "Jesus does not have thought (a term that for him corresponded more or less to 'spirit') like Papa; he has thought like God."

Capacity to See the Invisible

It is a fact that the child seems capable of seeing the Invisible, almost as if it were more tangible and real than the immediate reality. Bianca (five and a half years old) was mixing flour with yeast, as an exercise relating to the parable that compares the Kingdom of God to the yeast that leavens the dough. The catechist asked her to explain to a woman who had come to visit the center what she was doing; Bianca responded: "I am watching how the Kingdom of God grows."

A group of children between the ages of six and seven were meditating together with the catechist on Baptism as the participation in the life of the risen Christ. All the children were holding little candles in their hands that had been lit from the paschal candle, symbol of the risen Christ. The catechist wanted to help the children's meditation and spoke about the beauty of that "light" they had received, but Agnese constantly corrected her, saying: "It isn't light; it's goodness," as if the goodness were more visible to her than the light itself. Children penetrate effortlessly beyond the veil of signs and "see" with utmost facility their transcendent meaning, as if there were no barrier between the visible and the Invisible.

Capacity for Prayer ...

It is a fact that children have an extraordinary capacity for prayer, as regards duration as well as spontaneity and dignity of expression. Theirs is a prayer of praise and thanksgiving, which expresses the nearness and transcendence of God at the same time. But we will speak more about this later (see chapter 7).

The "Metaphysical" Child

All that we have been able to observe over these years, whether directly or through collaborators and former students, leads us to consider the child as a "metaphysical" being (the phrase is not ours)[14] who moves with ease in the world of the transcendent and who delights in—satisfied and serene—the contact with God. "God and the child get along well together," was the habitual expression of Adele Costa Gnocchi, one of Maria Montessori's first collaborators.

If we were to venture an explanation of all this, we could perhaps say that, since the religious experience is fundamentally an expression of love, it corresponds in a special way to the child's nature. We believe that the child, more than any other, has need of love because the child himself is rich in love. The child's need to be loved depends not so much on a lack that requires filling, but on a richness that seeks something that corresponds to it. "The religious attitude," observes Mencarelli, "is not ... an exclusive response to a need. It is the structuring of the whole personality operative in one's relationship with God."[15] It seems to us that a confirmation of an assertion like this can be found in the conclusions reached by P. Alberoa Algarra following a long period of observation in the Adele Costa Gnocchi Children's House (Rome): namely, that a child who is blocked in whatever aspect of his behavior will find great difficulty in becoming involved in a religious experience.[16] Algarra observed that, as the children gradually became "normalized," they displayed greater religious interests and joined together with other children in manifestations of a religious character.

Therefore, it is not in a search for compensation that the child turns to God, but from a profound exigence within the child's nature. The child needs an infinite, global love, such as no human being is able to give him. No child, I believe, has ever been loved to the degree that he wanted and needed. For the child, love is more necessary than food; it has been scientifically proved.[17] In the contact with God the child experiences an unfailing love. And in the contact with God the child finds the nourishment his being requires, nourishment the child needs in order to grow in harmony. God—who is Love—and the child, who asks for love more than his mother's milk, thus meet one another in a particular correspondence of nature. The child, in the encounter with God, delights in the satisfaction of a profound exigence of his person, of an authentic exigence of life. In helping the child's religious life, far from imposing something that is foreign to him, we are responding to the child's silent request: "Help me to come closer to God by myself."

NOTES

1. Maria Montessori, *Spontaneous Activity in Education,* trans. Florence Simmonds (New York: Schocken Books, 1970), pp. 351–353. Italian Edition, *Autoeducazione* (Milano: Garzanti, 1962), pp. 308–309.

2. S. Gallo, *Genesi del sentimento religioso nell'infanzia.* (Roma: Paoline, 1955), pp. 109ff.

3. Julien Green, *To Leave before Dawn,* trans. Anne Green (New York: Harcourt, Brace & World, Inc., 1967), p. 8. French Edition, *Partir Avant Le Jour* (Paris: Bernard Grasset, 1963), p. 26.

4. Sr. Jeanne d'Arc, *Cuore in ascolto* (Roma: Sales, 1968), pp. 80ff.

5. O. Kroh, *Die Psychologie der Grundschulkindes* (Tübingen, 1928), p. 51.

6. J. M. Arago-Mitjans, *Psicologia religiosa e morale del bambino e del fanciullo* (Torino-Leumann: LDC, 1970), pp. 207–208.

7. Anne Marie van der Meer, *Uomini e Dio* (Alba: Paoline, 1964), pp. 16–18.

8. Padre Dimitri Dudko, "Parroco a Mosca. Conversazioni serali," Quaderni della *Rivista del Centro studi Russia cristiana* (Milano: 1976), pp. 144–145.

9. Maria Montessori and others, *The Child in the Church,* ed. E. M. Standing. (St. Paul, Minnesota: Catechetical Guild Educational Society, 1965), pp. 24ff. Italian Edition, *I bambini viventi nella Chiesa* (Napoli: Morano, 1922), pp. 14ff.

10. J. M. Arago-Mitjans, *op. cit.*, pp. 65, 134–135.

11. Other examples can be found in Gianna Gobbi and Sofia Cavalletti, *Teaching Doctrine and Liturgy* (New York: Society of St. Paul, 1966), pp. 54ff. Italian Edition, *Educazione religiosa, liturgia e metodo Montessori* (Roma: EP, 1961), pp. 39ff.

12. A. Nichols, "Parables for Primaries," *Religion Teacher's Journal* (May–June 1975), pp. 13ff.

13. Arago-Mitjans, *op. cit.*, pp. 133–135.

14. A. Frossard, *Le Figaro* (August 10, 1970): "There are none so truly metaphysical as children."

15. M. Mencarelli, *Metodologia, didattica e creatività* (Brescia: La Scuola, 1974), p. 524.

16. P. Alberoa Algarra, *op. cit.*, p. 76.

17. M. A. Ribble, *I diritti del vostro bambino* (Milano: Bompiani, 1943), see in particular pp. 14–19; H. F. Harlow-R. D. Dodsworth-G. L. Arling, "Maternal Behavior of Rhesus Monkeys Deprived of Mother and Peer Association in Infancy," *Proceedings of the American Psychological Society, 1976*, pp. 329–335.

Chapter Two
The Child and the Adult

"The one who makes himself as little as this little child is the greatest in the kingdom of heaven."

Matthew 18:4

In a document published by the Italian Episcopal Conference, it is stated: "The religious world of the child presents itself with a physiognomy all its own";[1] and G. Milanesi writes: "The religion of the child is specific; it cannot be evaluated in comparison with the religion of an adult."[2] The world of the child's religion is a different world from that of the adult. The adult no longer has that open and peaceful relationship with God which is natural to the child; for the adult, the religious life is sometimes strain and struggle. For the adult the immediate reality at times acts as a screen to the transcendent reality that seems to be so apparent to the child. And above all, the adult has lost in his relationship with God the essentiality that is one of the most characteristic aspects of the religious personality of the child. The younger the child the more capable he is of receiving great things, and the child is satisfied only with the great and essential things. The child's interior life is deeply serious and without trappings. Sartre also knew that children are serious persons: "Children hate childishness when among themselves; they are truly men."[3]

The essentiality of the child is perhaps the element that imposes the severest discipline on the adult. How many superstructures have we accumulated in our inner life! If we want to help the child draw nearer to God we should, with patience and cour-

47

age, unrelentingly strip ourselves of these superfluous elements, and seek to go always closer to the vital nucleus of things. This requires study and prayer. The child himself will be our teacher of essentiality, if we know how to observe him.

What then can the adult do, faced with a being who seems to live his relationship with God in a way that is so different from our own?

The Proclamation

The adult's task is certainly to initiate the child into certain realities. There are events at the basis of Christianity that the adult should make known; there is an inheritance of truth and values that the adult should transmit with the whole of his lived life, but also through the word. In other words, the adult should proclaim God, who reveals His love through His Christ; he should give the "kerygma."

When dealing with children we would in fact have to speak more of proclamation and evangelization than of catechesis; this is the time of the child's first impact with God's Word, and its presentation should have all the characteristics proper to the kerygma.[4] The characteristic of the Judeo-Christian religious stream is that it is founded on events: the God of the Jews and Christians manifests and communicates Himself in history, so that His Word cannot be understood merely by looking around us and admiring nature as in naturalistic religions, nor simply by living in a Christian environment. The community surrounding us is the indispensable support of a Word that must be transmitted to us, and it is the necessary soil that receives that Word; however, living in such soil cannot be a substitute for the message.

The Christian is born into and grows within the community of believers who lean forward together in the listening to God, who speaks to His creatures. "Listen, Israel . . ." are words addressed to ancient Israel, which are still valid today in the Christian field as well.[5] "The proclamation," observes D. Grasso, "is an essential phase of preaching, which can be delayed after baptism but not omitted."[6] Thus the proclamation should constantly vivify every discussion, as a "point of reference and stimulus of renewal" to avoid the danger of falling into an arid and conceptualized transmission of religious truths.[7]

The Receivers of the Proclamation

The receivers of the kerygma are the child *and* the adult; they are simultaneously announcers and listeners. The proclamation is indeed necessary to the child, who is coming to know new things. However, it is also necessary for the adult, who needs to penetrate always more deeply into those things that often remain on the surface, who needs to continually enliven that which risks losing the vivacity of its first encounter in his life. To give the proclamation does not mean to take the position of a teacher, but only to offer a particular service. Nonetheless, it is a service that does not alter what should be the constant attitude of the person facing the Word of God: the attitude of a person who opens oneself, with joy, wonder, and gratitude, before a gift that reveals itself to be always greater.

It can be extremely stimulating for the adult who places himself in a position of listening together with the community of children, for they will easily involve the adult in that wondrous admiration which is characteristic of young children. Children will help the adult to recover certain aspects of the message and to keep awakened certain vital wellsprings within himself. Thanks to the children, the sense that the relationship with God is first of all one of joy will stay especially alive in the adult, and the adult will be enabled to free himself from some somber aspects characteristic of a particular formation, which perhaps is not yet completely overcome in our time.

Listening in community is always enriching. Listening with children is especially so, in our estimation, because God's Word resounds in a different manner in young children than in adults, and thus it is through children that another nuance of the Word reaches us. This will happen, however, on the condition that the catechist does not succumb to the temptation of assuming the attitude of a teacher, but rather the attitude of one who is open to listening, and who is not forgetful that one may speak only in the measure that one listens.

This openness to listening is a fundamental educative element for children and adults. Listening is the leaning toward others, the opening of ourselves in a receptive attitude toward the reality around us; it is only the capacity to listen that prevents us from revolving around ourselves. As for the child, we think that there is no age when the person is more capable of lis-

tening than in early childhood. The adult must struggle to attain
that "simple and humble" listening which is necessary, according to Cullmann, to approach God's Word.[8] The adult finds it
hard to receive the Word for itself, to remove all preoccupations
from his mind and heart. In the adult, the space of acceptance is
never whole; yet it is in the child. The child is really capable of
listening impartially and unselfishly, and so the child is receptive to the greatest degree. Early childhood presents itself therefore as a privileged age for accepting the kerygma.

The Content of the Proclamation

Having established the openness of the child, the elements of
the proclamation that are to be given to the child remain to be
seen. That the child is a being especially open to listening does
not mean that he will receive everything, and still less does it
mean that anything whatsoever can be the nourishment capable
of appeasing the "hunger" the child manifests.

If the child, as we have said, lives in a religious world all his
own, the adult, in making the proclamation, cannot take himself
as the measure; the adult cannot plan his work at a desk, basing
it on his own personal experience and reactions. The adult
should place himself in an attitude of observation, waiting for
the child to indicate which are the elements of the Christian
message he most receives, which aspect of the face of God satisfies the needs of childhood. Maria Montessori has written some
beautiful pages on the teacher's attitude with respect to the student, highlighting the contrast between the solemn, aloof teacher who sits as one enthroned on high before an audience that
hears without joining in, and the learned scientist who, mingling
with the students, observes with patience and love the phenome-
na of life.[9] The latter is the attitude the educator should acquire.
The catechist who knows how to observe the child will realize
that it is the greatest and most essential of realities that the
child seeks, in which the child delights and is appeased. A three-
and-a-half year old boy had already heard the Good Shepherd
parable when someone spoke to him of the guardian angel, explaining that it is an angel that the Lord gives to protect us; the
child (*sit venia verbis*) observed: "What do I need an angel for? I
have the Good Shepherd." Between two figures that both express
God's protective love, the child did not hesitate to choose the
greater.

We should be aware that frequently we are not sufficiently serious with children, that we do not give these "grown-ups" food that is adequately "adult"; it is enough to count the times we feel we ought to use diminutives with children. We cannot deny that it is precisely the greatest realities that we neglect to give the child; we hardly touch on them, taking them for granted. However, we should ask ourselves if it is actually superfluous to announce that God is unfailing love, that Christ is truly risen. To what degree are we ourselves convinced of these realities?

Moreover, there is the conviction, often unexpressed verbally, that the child is not capable of receiving such great realities. I believe the truth to be otherwise: It is we who have not managed to transmit these realities to children with that essentiality which is necessary, and the assumed incapacity of the child becomes an excuse to cover our ignorance and to exempt us from further and deeper research. It is easier and less demanding for us to speak to the child about a guardian angel than of Christ, Who died and is risen. Theology, in the serious sense of the word, is not knowledge for the elite. Every time we are unable to transmit theology to children or the uneducated, we should question ourselves, and we will come to realize, as we go closer to the core of things, that our inability depends on our own ignorance. How many times were we aware that we were not succeeding in speaking to the children about the greatest realities (how much difficulty we experienced with the Mass!) because we were unable to proclaim them with the essentiality the children needed. Only little by little, as we managed to go to the heart of things, were we able to communicate them to young children.

We should not be afraid to approach the greatest themes with the youngest children, but we should do so on an abstract level. As long as we are able to stay on a plane of essentiality, the children will listen to us, enchanted, happy, and never tiring; as soon as we leave this level, their attention will abandon us. Maria Montessori gave as a rule for her teachers the words of Dante: "Le parole tue sian conte," "Let your words be counted." May our words be few, but great in weight, above all with the youngest children. It is necessary for us to concentrate on a few, essential themes, not only to respond to the children's needs, but also to give them something that is able to grow along with them; that is, a vital nucleus that can open itself to ever widening horizons and, as such, something that can constitute the foundation for the future religious life of the older child and adult.

The Adult as "Unworthy Servant"

The adult who is to proclaim the most essential points of the Christian message, to listen to it with the children, and to observe the children in order to know their needs should remind himself that he is the "unworthy servant" of the Gospel. The adult's function as a mediator is necessary in evangelization; nonetheless it should not be overvalued. The catechist proclaims a Word that is not one's own and assists the child's potentialities, which in no way belong to oneself. The adult cannot help but recognize how often the results surpass the promises of one's work. The adult is so often made aware of the disproportion between what one has given and what the children manifest to possess and to live. At times our hands touch the presence of an active force that is not ours, and it is precisely because it is not our own that it fills us with wonder and deep joy. There is a deep bond uniting God to the child, the Creator to His creature; it is a bond that cannot be explained as the result of any human work, a bond with which no person should dare to interfere.

The catechist's task is to create specific conditions so that this relationship may be established, but to withdraw as soon as the contact occurs. We should take the greatest care not to intervene between God and the child with our encumbering person, with our insistent words. The adult's meditation is a service that is offered to the Word of God and to the child, and it has all the limitations of a service. The catechist who does not know when to stop, who does not know how to keep silent, is one who is not conscious of one's limits and, after all, is lacking in faith, because, on the practical level at least, one is not convinced that it is God and His creative Word that are active in the religious event. The help the adult can give the child is only preliminary and peripheral, and one that halts—that must halt—on the threshold of the "place" where God speaks with His creature.[10] Saint Thomas states that "the teacher only brings exterior help, as the physican who heals"; the teacher's task is that of the person who "proposes aids and tools."[11] On this subject Thomas cites Boethius: "Through teaching, the mind is stimulated to know; but the one who stimulates the other to know is not capable of making the other know, just as the person who stimulates the eye to see is incapable of making the eye see."[12]

In the process of the knowledge of and encounter with God, there is a second and more precious moment that follows the adult's exposition, a moment made of silence, for it is the time in which the listening becomes interior. During this moment the child reconsiders within himself what has been presented, in an intimate conversation with the Teacher within. Saint Augustine speaks of this:

> But all these branches of learning, which teachers profess to teach ... when they have explained them by means of words; then they who are called pupils, consider in the inner court of the mind whether what has been said is true, that is, in the measure of their own mental power they see the truth that is within. Then, therefore, they learn.[13]

The incandescent moment of the meeting with God occurs in secret between the Lord and His creatures, and into this secret the adult may not and should not enter.

Indirect Aid: The Sources

There is still another aid the adult can give the child, even during the time of inner listening; however, it must be a distant and indirect aid so as not to distract the child from his dialogue with the true Master, and so as not to allow the adult undue interference. To achieve this aim the adult should give the child, before all else, a way to have direct access to the sources, namely, to the scriptural and liturgical texts. The biblical and liturgical texts should not be found only in the catechist's hands, but also in the hands of the child. In saying this I obviously do not mean biblical or liturgical texts in their entirety; I mean passages that are complete in themselves.

It is not sufficient to give single verses of this or that text for a personal meditation. If, for example, we were to present the Good Shepherd parable to children, we would then have to provide them with a way of remaining on their own, one to one with the text of the *whole* parable, so that they could pursue their own personal meditation in it. God's Word has many aspects and resounds in each person in a unique way: if we limit ourselves to giving the child one or two verses of our choice, verses that best express the parable's teaching in our opinion, we intervene unduly between the text and the child, imposing on the child *our* experience with the text, *our* way of listening to it. A single verse may say many things to one who knows the passage in its entirety, to one who can synthesize a long familiarity with a whole text into those few words. But the text can remain totally silent to the person who has not had the same experience.

The text is alive when it is complete: By presenting this or that line to the child we claim for ourselves the incandescent moment of the direct encounter with the living Word; we deny the child the originating moment of that experience. We supply the child with a product we have already worked out and, as such, one that is limited, rather than opening up the boundless realm of God's Word before the child. The child cannot meditate on a single verse; at most he can learn it and repeat it through a process of superficial learning that is academic rather than vital in nature. The single verse will not enter deeply into the child's heart, and it will not inflame his life. To give the child direct access to the sources means to position the child in a state of independence from us, thereby helping him to establish a personal relationship with the Word of God; it is to make possible and incite the child's personal meditation, the dialogue with the interior Master.

Indirect Aid: The Material

There is also another indirect aid the adult can give the child in relation to the meditation following the proclamation, and that is the material.

According to Maria Montessori's conception, the material is not understood as an aid to the teacher but as a help for the child.[14] In the Montessori method there is a sensorial material the purpose of which is to develop the senses, and a cultural material that tends toward abstraction. The catechetical material corresponds fundamentally to the Montessori material in general: It is a means of rendering the child independent of the adult, in that it enables the child to reflect, on his own, on what has been presented; it is a way of letting the child prolong, alone with the inner Teacher, the meditation begun together with the adult. Nevertheless, there is a difference: The catechetical material is not designed to lead to abstraction but to the vital knowledge of a concrete Person; it does not lead to the consideration of ideas but to prayer; it is not only an aid to learning but a help for one's

religious life as well. Material that does not meet these require-
ments would not be good material.

Evidently the adult is still present, in some way, in the material itself, since he prepared it. Indeed, the material should be
yet another manifestation of the adult's love for God's Word. But
the work the child does with the material allows the adult to
make his presence more discreet, it permits him to take a secondary position so that the Word of God stands out as sovereign.

The catechetical material is not comprised of abstract symbols, as is the material relating to grammar, for example; instead
it consists of concrete "signs" of a transcendent reality. The material for catechesis is nothing else than the transposition, into a
more tangible and didactically graduated form, of what is found
in the Bible and Liturgy. The material for Baptism, for instance,
is composed of the liturgical "signs"* of the sacrament presented
to the child in gradual succession, as will be seen later; there is
nothing more—and there need not be anything more—than
what is found in the Liturgy. This is equally true for the parable
material, about which we will say more later on; there should be
the details of the parable and only these.

The catechist who wants to prepare material for catechesis
need not invent anything. The catechist need only know in depth
the elements he wishes to actualize, and to concretize it in a way
that is most faithful to the sources and most essential in form.
Material that is the catechist's own personal invention, or that
does not reproduce in its essentiality the biblical or liturgical element it is intended to represent, is not good material. The catechist who feels obligated to invent should question himself; perhaps he does not know well what he is attempting to achieve.
Good material is simple, essential, and immediate. The catechist's creativity does not consist in a kind of creation out of
nothing, but in always probing more deeply into the treasures of
God's Word and in presenting them in such a way as to give
space to the child's creativity.

---

*Both Italian and English are inconsistent in the usage of "sign" as opposed to
the word "symbol." Often Cavalletti uses "sign" to indicate an open and participating indicator of reality that can have many levels of interpretation. In English we usually call this linguistic function the work of a symbol. With this
warning the reader can consult the context of usage to sharpen the meaning Cavalletti intends. Another word, "images," will be added to this when she speaks
of the prophecies.

Indirect Aid: The Environment

The preparation of the environment is another indirect aid the adult should give the child. This is a fundamental principle in the Montessori method, the importance of which all modern psychology points out. The "atrium" is the name Maria Montessori gave to the environment dedicated to the child's religious life, recalling that space in the ancient Christian basilicas which served as the anteroom of the church, both in the material and metaphorical sense of the word. Montessori intended the atrium to be an intermediate place between the classroom and the church. It is a place where the child comes to know the great realities of his life as a Christian, but also and above all, a place where the child begins to live these realities in meditation and prayer. There is nothing of the academic classroom about the atrium; it is not a place for religious instruction but for religious *life*. The atrium is a place of work, where the work however becomes conversation with God. It is already in some manner a place of worship, where the child can live worship according to his own rhythm, which is not possible in a church. It is the place for the community of children and their catechists, and thus it is distinct from a church, which is the meeting place for the whole family of God.

The atrium may be compared to a retreat house; as such it should be a place that facilitates recollection and silence, even in its external aspects of wall decorations and other furnishings. It is desirable that the atrium be "Mass-centered," that is, a place where special prominence is awarded to the material relative to the Mass; a place where the baptismal font stands out in the area assigned to Baptism. The Gospel should have a position of honor and be located alongside the parable materials and materials relating to the historical life of Christ (in the atrium for older children there should be the complete Bible).

There should be an area for prayer as well, especially in the atrium for the young children. The decorations in the prayer area should be changed following the progression of the liturgical year; the children themselves may prepare a colored covering for table or wall that corresponds to the liturgical season; a small kneeler or chair may invite the child to lengthen his stay there.

The catechist presents the individual themes in the area of the atrium containing the material for that subject. After the exposition of the materials, the catechist may gather the children together in the prayer area when the meeting is to be invested with special solemnity, particularly as the great feasts of Christmas, Easter, and Pentecost draw near.

To offer an idea of the atmosphere that can be created in an atrium, we quote the following passages from the unpublished diary of a catechist from Colonna (Rome):

> One by one I say all the children's names: "Jesus told the parable for Gianfranco . . ." Little by little as I speak slowly, solemnly and with long pauses, the silence grows always deeper and more intense. Each sentence I say more solemnly and softly, and I feel vividly and almost tangibly that it is God's voice speaking to me and the children through my own voice. These are unique and moving experiences for me.

Another section from the same diary:

> I take the material of the Publican and the Pharisee parable, and I narrate it. The silence is profound. You can feel the soul of each child is eager, attentive and at the same time full of peace; it is the distinct sensation I always have in meeting with the children when the moment comes to proclaim the Word of God (and they are tremendous, unrestrained forces of nature). It happens regularly: pencils are put down or stay suspended in the air (usually I do not have the children move from their places); each child peacefully turns toward me and makes himself comfortable and relaxed. This phenomenon has recurred regularly since the beginning of the year; every time I feel deeply moved and peaceful at the same time. If Jesus were to enter through the closed door and sit down among us, I would not be more amazed than I am at this intense disposition toward listening in our young children. Actually, it really is like that: Jesus, risen and glorious, enters through the closed door to speak once again the same words as then, to speak to us, people of today, who live in time, in the present without past and without future, which is the time of God. And this overwhelming, invisible presence

of His is so strong that suddenly I am no longer afraid of
ruining God's words by repeating them. My voice will
pass through His Person, present though invisible, and
will bring to each child the light and love each needs in
that moment. It will be His light and His love (no longer
my words) that will go forth. I must try to explain this
thought to the other catechists so they may become
more aware of this and also have more courage to speak.

The following is quoted from the unpublished diary of a catechist from the parish of San Francesco in Rome:

While a group (children from five to six years old) are
working with the liturgical calendar, Leonardo and I get
the Good Shepherd material. The others leave their
drawings and come close to us. I recount the parable and
each child moves a sheep. They are happy to repeat ad
infinitum: "The Good Shepherd knows his sheep and the
sheep know his voice," "he calls them . . ." and each
child says his name and moves a sheep. After more than
a half-hour of this work they dictate their prayers to me,
which we say afterwards in church. The visit is joyful
and *full of peace.* Then Leonardo (who disturbs the others because he wants to touch everything—I am beginning to think that really young children are listening
when they are touching, that is, they are reliving) and I
go to work at the miniature altar. His self-possessed joy
and his desire to control his movements are incredible. I
am learning to do everything within long periods of
time, with long pauses, with extremely slow gestures.
There is a deep peace around us and I believe also within the children; it is certainly within me. They do not
want to leave. Gabriella is on the verge of tears; we have
a long talk about what we will do next time, what she
will do, what the other children will do. Gradually the
tears subside and peace returns at this great hope: what
we are going to do the next time. Her mother, very dis-
concerted herself, helped in this scene.

A group of children (Canada) spontaneously decided to give
the atrium names of their own making. They requested that

their drawings, with accompanying names, be placed on the outside of the atrium door. Some of the names were:

"The pearl."
"The room of joy."
"Our room is very beautiful."
"This room is like bread growing."
"I think our room is the room of love and God."
"This room is about God and Jesus and the Holy Spirit."
"This room is like a mustard seed."

If the atrium is in the school, it will have its first natural
sphere of resonance in the school itself, where often there are
children whose families have very different convictions regarding religion. In an especially difficult class, where an atmosphere
of understanding and collaboration had not been established, a
little girl remarked that, from the time several of the children
started going to the atrium to prepare for first communion, "an
atmosphere of greater love was born." The atrium therefore is a
place where the child has certain experiences of a religious nature, which do not stay within the confines of the atrium itself.
This has been attested by many parents who, through their children, were opened to new religious horizons and also by numerous children who were drawn to attend the Catechetical Center
by their own peers.

The Community

And so the adult has many demanding tasks to accomplish if
he wants to help the child to live his relationship with God. All
that we have tried to describe is very important and necessary in
our opinion; however, in all this, the adult's task is still not finished. The adult should prepare an environment for the child, in
the exact sense of a place but also and especially an environment
in the wider significance of the word, meaning the community of
faith. In the atrium the child is already living a community life,
as we have mentioned; yet it is one that is restricted to the community of children, which cannot be sufficient, particularly as
the child begins to grow. The seed of God's Word, which the child
receives, has need of the *"hortus conclusus"* (secret garden) of the
atrium, and also the supportive oxygen of the adult community.

One cannot substitute for the other: One integrates the other in a complementary function that is inseparable and without substitute.

In the absence of a faith environment where the child may live, of which he feels himself a part and in which he feels himself almost held, we risk cultivating hothouse flowers in the atrium, which are incapable of enduring the severity of the external climate. On the other hand, without a place where the child can come in touch with the religious reality in a way and at a rhythm suitable to children, there is the danger the child will pass by great things without ever being able to grasp, interiorize, and make these realities his own. The initiation of a child into Christian life is not a work that can be fulfilled by the catechist alone, nor by the parents alone. It is the whole Christian community that proclaims Christ, and the child must enter into contact with the entire Christian community. The catechist's work—valuable as it is—must be sustained and confirmed by a community that lives what the catechist proclaims.[15]

NOTES

1. Italian Episcopal Conference, *Il Rinnovamento della Catechesi* (Roma: 1970), n. 135.
2. G. Milanesi, *Psicologia della religione* (Torino-Leumann: LDC, 1974), p. 76.
3. J. P. Sartre, *Les mots* (Paris: Gallimard, 1964), p. 165: "Les enfants entre eux haïssent les enfantillages; ils sont des hommes pour vrai."
4. E. Alberich, *Natura e compiti di una catechesi moderna* (Torino-Leumann: LDC, 1972), pp. 133–140; D. Grasso, *L'annuncio della salvezza* (Roma: Paoline, 1965), p. 330.
5. For the importance of the education of the capacity to listen see Sofia Cavalletti, "L'educazione nella Bibbia a nel Talmud" in *Nuove questioni di storia della pedagogia*, Vol. 1 (Editrice La Scuola, 1977), pp. 13–15.
6. D. Grasso, "Il Kerigma e la predicazione," *Gregorianum* (1960), p. 435. For the importance of the cognitive element in religious formation, see also D. Silvestri, "L'educazione religiosa nell'infanzia, oggi" *Rassegna di Pedagogia* (1975), pp. 49–56.
7. On the use of postbaptismal catechesis in ancient tradition see Jean Daniélou and R. Du Charlat, *La catéchèse aux pre-*

miers siècles, (Paris: Fayard-Mame, 1968), p. 44. Italian Edition, *La catechesi nei primi secoli* (Torino-Leumann: LDC, 1968), pp. 34ff.

8. O. Cullmann, *Christus und die Zeit* (Zurich: 1962), p. 25; J. Robinson and E. Fuchs, *La nuova ermeneutica* (Brescia: Paideia, 1967), p. 65: "Where there is listening to and acceptance of the call of being, there is man."

9. Maria Montessori, *Spontaneous Activity in Education,* pp. 125–141. Italian Edition, *Autoeducazione,* pp. 111–119; A. M. Joosten, "Learning from the Child," Inaugural Addresses of the XXV and XXVI Indian Montessori Training Courses (Hyderabad, 1962).

10. On this subject see A. M. Joosten, "On Christian Education," *Word and Worship,* 2 (1970), pp. 1–12.

11. Saint Thomas Aquinas, *Summa Theologica Vol. I,* Q. 117, a.1 in *The "Summa Theologica" of St. Thomas Aquinas Part I, Vol. 5* (London: Burns Oates & Wasbourne, Ltd., 1941), pp. 178–179.

12. Saint Thomas Aquinas, *De Veritate,* Q. XI, no. 12, passim: Boethius, *De Consolatione Philosophiae (The Consolation of Philosophy) Book V,* 5.

13. Saint Augustine, *De Magistro,* XIV, 45, in *The Philosophy of Teaching:* A Study in the Symbolism of Language, A Translation of St. Augustine's "De Magistro," trans. Father Francis E. Tourscher (Pennsylvania: Villanova College, 1924), p. 90.

14. Maria Montessori, *The Discovery of the Child,* trans. Mary A. Johnstone (India, Kalakshetra Publications, 1966), pp. 136–143. Italian Edition, *La mente del bambino* (Milano: Garzanti, 1952), pp. 181–182.

15. This is a constant theme in the documents of the Second Vatican Council, in particular *Dei Verbum* and *Lumen Gentium*; it is also emphasized in *Il Rinnovamento della Catechesi,* no. 182ff. in particular.

Chapter Three
Christ the Good Shepherd

"The Lord is my shepherd."
Psalm 23:1

The adult who accepts the silent request of the child: "Help me to come closer to God by myself," must choose the way to give the child the help he asks for. We are faced with three possibilities: catechesis may be theocentric, Christocentric, or anthropocentric.

Christocentric Catechesis and Parable

Theocentric catechesis begins by speaking of the Father as Creator and arrives at Christ at a later time; this method follows the historical development of revelation. However, we ask ourselves if a Christian child should not be initiated first into that relationship with God which is truly Christian, that is, the relationship with the Father through His incarnate Son. We wonder if in this first method, which seems to be more attentive to the reality of history, there may not be perhaps a certain deficiency of the historical sense. We know that from the Incarnation onward a particular bond was established between man and God that was sealed in the flesh of the Son; we know that Christ is the unique mediator: "I am the door" (John 10:9); "No one can come to the Father except through me" (John 14:6).

It seems to us that the theocentric foundation does not take adequate account of the great event of the Incarnation and the fact that, after it, man's situation with God is truly changed—and we must take such a change into consideration, we have to pass through Christ who constituted Himself as mediator. It is

62

through Christ, "the way," that we go to the Father. In our view, this is the kind of foundation still found in those catechisms that begin their consideration of God as the one who reveals Himself in the works of creation, and only at a later time do they come to speak of Christ.

We will wait until later to clarify if, and in what sense, the method we follow may be defined as anthropocentric, seeking as it does to satisfy the needs within the inmost part of the child (see chapter eleven). Here we would like to elucidate the importance the person of Christ can have in the child's religious life, and to describe how we have presented Him to children.[1]

In regard to Christ we also find ourselves faced with a choice: whether to center the proclamation on the history of His life by following its development from His birth to His resurrection, or to initiate the child more directly into the mystery of the person of Christ and His relationship with us, in the form of the parable.

The children's reaction to this second approach has demonstrated to us once again that it is only the greatest realities that correspond to the needs of the youngest children; their response has made us experience personally how capable they are of piercing beyond the images into the metaphysical reality. Although our catechesis closely follows the liturgical year, and thus chronologically we begin to speak about Christ starting with His birth, the central element of the proclamation we give to younger children consists in the parable-allegory of the Good Shepherd (John 10:1–16). The central element in the catechesis for the older children is the other great Johannine parable-allegory, the True Vine (15:1–10).

The Essentials of the Proclamation to Children

Our sequence of presentation follows the rhythm of the life of the Church, which, according to the liturgical seasons, highlights various aspects of Christ's life; that is, it traces the liturgical year, so that catechesis becomes an actual part of the life being lived by the Church.

The outline we offer provides for at least a two-year period. The writing in the direction of the circle indicates the subjects that are divided into separate years: the innermost part of the circle comprises the subjects to be presented to the children in the first year, those in the outermost part of the circle are pre-

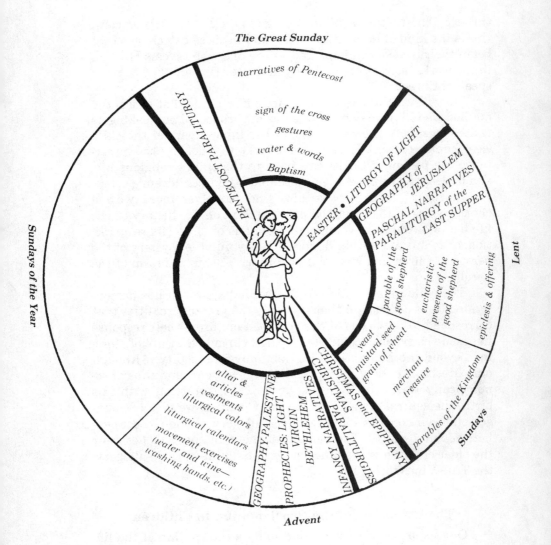

The Great Sunday

narratives of Pentecost

sign of the cross

gestures

water & words

Baptism

PENTECOST PARALITURGY

EASTER • LITURGY OF LIGHT

GEOGRAPHY of JERUSALEM

PASCHAL NARRATIVES
PARALITURGY of the LAST SUPPER

parable of the good shepherd

eucharistic presence of the good shepherd

epiclesis & offering

Lent

yeast
mustard seed
grain of wheat

merchant treasure

parables of the Kingdom

Sundays

Sundays of the Year

altar & articles
vestments
liturgical colors
liturgical calendars

movement exercises
(water and wine—
washing hands. etc.)

GEOGRAPHY-PALESTINE
PROPHECIES: LIGHT
VIRGIN
BETHLEHEM

INFANCY NARRATIVES
CHRISTMAS and EPIPHANY
CHRISTMAS PARALITURGIES

Advent

sented during the second year. The writing perpendicular to the circle indicates the themes that are repeated, although in a slightly different form, each year.

In the following chapters we will develop each of these themes in detail, describing how we present them to the children and their reactions to them, and offering our reflections on the children's response. In this more thorough examination it will become apparent how these individual themes form a unity in which each element is complete in itself and at the same time prepares for further development. It will also become clear that the Good Shepherd parable is the cornerstone of all this work: It is linked to the Eucharistic presence, the infancy and paschal narratives, the Easter liturgy of light, and the sacrament of baptism.

The Presentation of the Parable

We present the Good Shepherd to children according to the method we usually use for parables, that is to say, with the greatest respect for the text, without adding anything other than what is found there. I do not think that such a text, which is so rich theologically and so literarily valuable, needs embellishment or additions on our part. We restrict ourselves to highlighting the parable's various elements, and to helping the children savor their richness. The Good Shepherd parable (or allegory if one prefers) is a complex text with multiple images; some elements require a certain historical knowledge of the time in which Jesus lived in Palestine in order to be comprehended (e.g., the person who does not enter the sheepfold by the gate). Therefore we necessarily postpone the presentation of verses 1–3a and 7–10a until later, concentrating on those elements that have most impact on the children. If we are working with very young children, from two-and-a-half to four years of age, it is advisable not to mention the wolf, and perhaps not even the hireling.

The points on which we linger, for it is these that most enchant the children, are above all the personal love and protective presence of the Good Shepherd: He calls each one of His sheep by name (fig. 6), He knows each intimately even if there are many sheep; He calls his sheep and gradually they become accustomed to the voice of their Good Shepherd and they listen to Him. In this way a precious relationship is established; a thread of love binds the sheep always more closely to their Shepherd. The

Shepherd's voice is powerful and supremely patient; it never tires of calling and reaches out even to those sheep who are far away, beyond the sheepfold. Slowly they too turn to hear His voice and they gather together into one great flock. The Shepherd knows the needs of His sheep, and He guides them to good pastures, walking ahead of them to show the way and to be the first to confront any danger should it arise. So the sheep are safe and peaceful with their Good Shepherd; they know there is someone to protect them even in danger.

As a further example of the Good Shepherd's love we may add the parable of the found sheep (Luke 15:4–6). Children under six years of age do not grasp the moral aspect of this parable because they are unaware of the whole problematic of sin and conversion. The catechist should be careful not to present the parable to children from this point of view; it would expose the presentation to sure failure and prevent the children from relishing the aspect that is most striking to them: the Good Shepherd's love is such that He cannot bear to know that even one of His sheep is alone and unprotected. So He goes in search of it, calling for it until His voice reaches the sheep, and sheep and Shepherd are together once again; even more, now the sheep is on the Good Shepherd's shoulders, now the sheep can go where He goes, and who could harm a sheep in the arms of its Shepherd?

Community Meditation on the Parable

When we have recounted the content of the parable, we then begin a communal meditation on its elements. An aspect that is not immediately clear to the children is that we are the sheep; we should take great care not to explain this. We would deprive the children of the joy of the discovery. If they do not understand right away they will later on; the essential is that they come to the discovery themselves.[2] We should not be in a hurry; we know the time of the Spirit is slow.

The meditation following the parable narration should serve the catechist in reconsidering the text once more—with love and increasing wonder at its unfathomability—and also serve to help the children in discovering it. To encourage the children to join in the meditation, the catechist poses a number of questions without ever answering them, for example: "The Good Shepherd's sheep are so fortunate! They are so protected, defended, and loved! Do you think Jesus was speaking about the sheep we see in the fields?" Sometimes the children will answer "yes"; then, without yielding to the temptation to explain, it is best to continue: "Do you think so? I do not know. They are such important sheep. The Good Shepherd gives his very life for them," and so on.

If a child suddenly grasps the meaning and responds that we are the sheep, we can continue the discussion all the same: "You think the sheep are people? What do you think? And you? Then do we know the names of some of the Good Shepherd's sheep? Does the Shepherd call Francesco by name? Maria? How beautiful it is to be one of His sheep! How lucky we are!" and so on.

After the children have begun to understand that we are faced with a text that hides something to be discovered, then we read the parable with great solemnity. If by this time the children have already reached a point of penetration of the text, then frequently the reading will be followed by spontaneous prayer.

Personal Meditation

The material still remains to be presented, that is, the aid to the child's personal meditation. The material is comprised of small wooden figures. It is advisable that the figures be made with the facial characteristics only slightly accented, in order to distinguish them from the material relative to the historical part of the catechesis (we will say more about this later). Parables are the concretization of a suprasensible reality in an image; for our part, we have concretized this image in small figures of wood. We present the material elements (in this case, the Good Shepherd, the sheep, sheepfold, etc.) and then, as we reread the parable, we move the figures corresponding to the text. In this way the children learn how to use the material, which is then left at their disposal.

For the whole of the first year the children will return to work with this material, concentrated and happy, never satiated. If they know how to read, they work for the most part in pairs: one child reads* the text, the other moves the figures; taking the

---

*Cavalletti is assuming an open-graded classroom. In addition to the 3–6 year old children there are older children who can help with this if the younger ones do not know how to read. The children are not made to feel ashamed if they cannot read. Furthermore, Italian is a very phonetic language. Children often learn to read quite early, much as English-speaking children learn to read in easy readers where the phonograms so prevalent in our language have been artificially deleted.

part of manipulating the figures at the right time makes the child follow the reading with utmost attention and quite soon the child will know the passage by heart. If the children are very young and do not yet know how to read, they tell the parable to themselves and move the characters at the same time.

This is the second and most valuable moment of awareness, which we spoke of earlier: It is the time of the conversation with the inner Teacher, when the child reconsiders, without the adult, what has been presented and enters into its meaning. See drawing number 5; a child (five years old) brought his finished drawing to the catechist and she asked him: "Why did you put two children in the middle of the sheep?" (Notice the heart above each sheep, symbol of love.) The child responded: "Because as I was drawing I understood that we are the sheep." The child had not caught the significance of the image of the sheep while the catechist was speaking to him but only afterward during his own personal meditation.

This is the time when the child repeats the details of the parable to himself and absorbs them. For instance, a four-and-a-half year old child led the sheep one by one out of the fold and placed them behind the Good Shepherd; each time a sheep left the fold, the child took the Good Shepherd figure and turned it around momentarily so that it faced the sheep. The catechist observed the child without disturbing him. When he was finished working, she asked him why he had done it that way and the child replied: "He is calling them by name." This element is so important to children that one child, when questioned about the most significant aspect of the miracle of the resurrection of Lazarus, responded: "That he calls him by name."

Another child (four years old) asked himself in a whisper: "Why do the sheep walk behind the Good Shepherd?" and he answered himself, still whispering: "Because he is God." After a little girl (five years old) heard it read that the Good Shepherd walks ahead of the sheep and they follow because they know His voice, she took the figure of the Shepherd in one hand and a sheep in the other and had them walk closely together all around the sheepfold. Then she put the first sheep back in the fold and repeated the same action with all the others, one by one. At one point a sheep fell on the floor, and the child stooped down to pick it up with the Good Shepherd figure.

At times the children's interpretations are most personal: "There will be one flock and one shepherd," and Pier Marco (four years old) put even the wolf and hireling in the fold; his companions objected and tried to take the intruders away but Pier Marco explained: "But don't you understand that with the Good Shepherd everyone becomes good?" And a little two-and-a-half year old girl placed the hireling (the wolf had not been presented to her) behind the Good Shepherd and remarked: "Even he is good with the Good Shepherd; the Good Shepherd is just like my mother."

This is the moment when the child, in the inner dialogue, personalizes what has been presented and applies it to his own life. In the center there was a five-year-old boy from the outskirts of Rome; the railway passed alongside his suburb, a great danger to the children and the object of continual warnings from mothers. This child was using the Good Shepherd material; he followed a sheep that had wandered far away from the others and spoke to it in the Roman dialect: "Where are you going, ah crazy! Don't you know the train is there?" But the Shepherd arrived and carried the sheep to safety.

Slowly, as the children grow, they will use the material less, yet they continue to return to the text, often recopying it spontaneously many times and illustrating it. Only the older children (nine–ten years old) will sometimes stage and then perform the parable.

The Responsiveness of the Children

Numerous drawings and discussions, recorded in the children's own words, demonstrate how they enter the parable's message and how it resounds within them; the most apparent effect they derive from it is a serene peace, which is why they exclaim: "With the Good Shepherd everything is fine" (*si sta bene*), why they pray: "You are good because you guide us with goodness." The parable gives them a sense of feeling secure and protected: "Now I'm no longer afraid of anything; I go into my room when it's dark. I'm not afraid, because the Good Shepherd is always close to me" (five-year-old child). Paraphrasing the parable, a five-and-a-half year old boy wrote: "I am the Good Shepherd and I am the strongest." Another child, addressing the Shepherd, said: "You are powerful, you are strong"; but the Shepherd's strength is also ours: "Jesus goes to heaven with His own strength and the sheep go to heaven on Jesus' strength" (six-year-old child).

Nicola was an older child, seven years of age, and he had learned about the Good Shepherd parable from a person who spent a few days at his home. At a later time, Nicola visited someone else's house in another city; he was already in bed, but he called his aunt continually so she would reassure him with her presence. Then the child's tone of voice changed and he said to himself: "There is a great fence all around the world." Silence; then: "It is the Good Shepherd who pastures his sheep." More silence; and finally he said: "We are the sheep." And Nicola went to sleep peacefully, seeing the Good Shepherd's sheepfold in a cosmic projection and feeling himself to be part of it.

Drawing number 9 was done by a five-year-old girl who lived in an institution, virtually abandoned by her parents. She heard about the Good Shepherd and drew in the center of the sheet a "happy heart," her own! The Good Shepherd's love, even in the absence of parental love, was for her a gratifying experience. It has been noted by many catechists that often the children most lacking in human affection are the happiest in the encounter with the Good Shepherd. One could say therefore that the experience of His love need not necessarily be grafted onto an experience of human love, but that it is independent of it, uniting the child in a direct bond with God. Such an experience is rooted, perhaps, in that "sanctuary" within man where he finds himself "alone with God."[3]

Children who are sick or handicapped have a special sensitivity to the parable we are speaking about.[4] Maria, two years and ten months old, was being treated in the cancer ward of the Bambino Gesù pediatric hospital in Rome. She came from the south of Italy, so her parents lived far away. One cannot describe the sadness in her small, pale face nor the impossibility of establishing any rapport with her. "She is always on her own," related the other children, "sometimes she cries and cries but she says nothing." A catechist went to the hospital with the intention of speaking to Maria about the Good Shepherd's love, but her endeavors to make contact with the little girl seemed completely in vain. While the catechist presented the parable materials to a small group of children who had gathered around her bed, Maria appeared to be far away, if not actually asleep. However as the catechist read the parable, Maria's breathing became gradually calmer; when the catechist started to rise slowly from the chair beside her bed, Maria stood up abruptly, threw herself into the catechist's arms and kissed her. Discarding her doll, she cleared a space on her bed for the materials and indicated in an obvious way that she was waiting for a new presentation of the Good Shepherd. Then she took the parable book herself and suddenly began to say a number of things that unfortunately the catechist, who was a foreigner, could not understand. But communication had been established just the same: Maria wanted to be held in her arms, carried around the room, and fed when the dinner arrived. When it came time for the catechist to leave, Maria refused to let anyone else hold her and let her leave only after she promised to return the next day. The night nurse heard Maria singing softly: "He knows my name."

Alfonsito was twelve years old. He is a small, severely handicapped Mexican boy who had received a lot of medical care in his family, but very little love. By chance he happened to be visiting his aunt's home and he found the box, which was closed at the time, of the Good Shepherd material. What was it that urged Alfonsito to place his hand on that box saying: "Well?" At this indirect request of his, his aunt told him the parable briefly, for no longer than ten minutes, and then she showed him the material. Alfonsito seized it; he who had so much trouble in coordinating his movements took out one sheep after another, caressed and said to each: "Do not be afraid; you lack nothing." It was a great effort for him to pronounce the words because he had such difficulty with language. His concentration—for him it always had an extremely short span—this time lasted two hours with only one interruption, when the nurse came to make him do his exercises; at that point Alfonsito rebelled with an incredible violence so that he was left undisturbed. Then he went home in a tranquil state, something totally unusual because generally everything became a problem for him; "but," his mother said afterwards, "he kept saying strange words: 'Do not be afraid; you lack nothing.' "

Two days later the boy returned to his aunt's house; once again he found the box of parable material, put his hand on it and said: "Well?" This time his aunt told him the parable of the sheep that was lost, sought after with love, and found again. Around five minutes later Alfonsito made it known to his aunt that what she had said was sufficient. He began to work with the material once more, fondling each sheep, but this time he said: "I am not afraid; I lack nothing." Then, almost with pain at the start because of the enormous difficulty he had in speaking, something like a cry came from him and in a tone of voice that grew steadily he shouted: "He is for me alone! He is for me alone! He is for me alone!"

Alfonsito had finally found a love that was for him alone; and this changed his life. He never gave the parable material back to his aunt; he safeguarded it in the small cabinet with his other treasures, taking it out and carrying it with him on especially happy occasions. From that day on he was heard to sing now and then, and he managed, yet almost without words, to communicate his great secret to his younger brother.

This fact seems to confirm what we said earlier about the independence of the experience of God's love in regard to an experience of human love. Alfonsito is a boy little accepted by his family, nor did he have any special relationship with his aunt, whom he had not seen for some years until the day when he came to know the Good Shepherd. *After* that day a special bond was created between them.

One could object that at least the mediation of the catechist is necessary, and this is certainly true. But we are dealing precisely with a mediation, that is, a service rendered to the child so that he may enter into relationship with that source which puts him in peace. We ask ourselves what weight a catechist can have in the life of a child whom he meets for a short time, probably once or twice a week. It seems to us that the presence of the catechist or teacher—even the best catechist or teacher—could not be sufficient to give the child's life that affective base which is generally maintained to be necessary for a religious experience. The experience of the Good Shepherd's love—far from remaining empty and without a base when it is not linked to an affective life satisfied by human affection—is valid in itself.

The Affective Resonance of the Parable

In normal affective conditions, human feelings serve as a comparison to the Good Shepherd's love, to the total advantage of the latter. "Not even my brother knows everything about me; the Good Shepherd knows me by name" (seven-year-old child).

Among the various affective relationships the parable recalls, the maternal is prevalent. There are innumerable drawings in which a house is illustrated beside the sheepfold; the house, as psychology teaches us, is the image the child uses to refer to his mother (figs. 7, 16). This maternal reference also appears in their prayers and "little thoughts": "If I'm at home, I think of You, if I'm on the street I think of You; and when Mommy takes me by the hand, I think it's the Good Shepherd and I feel happy" (five-year-old child). Two children were speaking together; one child (three and a half) said: "The Good Shepherd is like my mother; he helps me, takes me across the street, he takes danger away," and the other child said: "Even if the wolf comes, Mommy will protect me." The drawing of Christopher John (two years, two months old; New Kensington, U.S.A.) is noteworthy from this point of view: Inside a red oval figure, with which he wanted to draw the Good Shepherd, he drew another smaller yellow oval, representing the sheep according to the child's explanation. Is there perhaps in this drawing a reference to the maternal womb?

The color yellow, which expresses joy, is often predominant in children's drawings, and frequently the semicircle appears, a sign of protection, security, and trust (figs. 10, 11).[5] A four-and-a-half year old boy explained why he had drawn flowers in a sheep's mouth: "He is so happy, Jesus takes him to beautiful places."

The maternal reference, even if it is very widespread among younger children, is not however exclusive. An inquiry was made in various groups of children; they were asked who among the persons closest to them most resembled the Good Shepherd. The majority of children identified the mother; a smaller number said the mother and father (in this order for the most part); fewer still replied the father; others answered, a friend, sister, brother, teacher, all the persons dearest to them; a little boy responded: "My younger sister." Thus it appears that the Good Shepherd relates to the child's entire affective range, and this fact seems to us to be another proof of the parable's wealth and yet another reason to make it the supportive pillar of all our catechesis.

The affective resonance of the Good Shepherd merits more extensive and detailed investigation. We wonder if it is the very fact that the Good Shepherd image does not correspond to any precise figure in the child's life that makes it so rich. Any particular reference can be limiting; if we speak of God as Father, the connection will be made with the human father exclusively, and the paternal image is probably not even the one that relates most fully to the young child's needs.[6] It is not difficult to imagine the damage the child will undergo, in the religious sense, whose father is quite the opposite of an ideal figure. However, since the Good Shepherd is open to an enormously vast affective range, the child will always find a loved person in whom he sees the reflection of the Good Shepherd's love.

In any case, the parable is so deeply rooted within the child that it appears to be natural in him. It returns constantly in the children's discussions, reflections, and prayer. The child does not know the parable in an academic way, but vitally; it is not knowledge imposed on the child from without; rather, it is through the parable that the child's silent request finds response and gratification: the request to be loved and so to be able to love. The child never forgets the parable because the affective integration, which psychologists call "affective ratification," is complete; the image of the Shepherd is by now a part of the child's very person. The affective integration is an element that is generally overlooked in catechesis, as the results of Vianello's research attest.[7] It is this kind of deficiency that causes what Vianello terms the "world-God fracture" and that often makes religious education for children from four to seven years of age appear like an "alien body," according to Piaget's observation.[8] Affectivity is more or less ignored to the advantage of the cognitive component, resulting in an arid and sterile knowledge that does not permeate the child's life.

Development According to Age

Once again we observe that the Good Shepherd parable is not restricted to satisfying the present needs of the child. Even in young children the parable begins, in flashes, to open them toward wider horizons; for example, the community dimension, which relates to the needs of the following age, is already present at times in early childhood. Commenting on his drawing, a young child wrote: "I love Jesus and I love his sheep too." Pier Marco, when asked what would happen if the lost sheep did not want to come back to the fold, resolved the problem by saying: "Then the Good Shepherd goes to get all the other sheep and they convince him to return. But the sheepfold is the church (except there isn't any grass)."

We need not be concerned about the prevalence of the maternal reference and hence about the aspect of enjoyment the Good Shepherd parable elicits. As we said, we think early childhood is primarily the time of the serene enjoyment of God. In saying this we do not thereby deny that the element of enjoyment, integrated with the other components, should always be present in the religious fact.[9] Furthermore, this parable has a starting date in the life of the young child but it does not have an end date in our life. Once begun, the relationship with the Good Shepherd never ceases; the parable will grow slowly with the child, revealing its other aspects and satisfying the needs of the older child, adolescent, and adult. We allude only to the fact that the child after six years of age begins to realize that the parable of the "found sheep" reveals how the Shepherd's protective love is a love that is forgiving as well; His love is really unfailing, it is inexhaustible even when confronted with wrong behavior. The older child, who in preadolescence is oriented toward heroic ideals, will see in the Shepherd who "walks ahead of His sheep" the person who shows us the path, one that is not without difficulties but that has as its aim the "superabundant" life of the risen Lord. The development is from the love that protects, to the love that forgives, and, finally, to the *imitatio Christi*. The parable fulfills in a specific way the exigencies peculiar to the three stages of development Maria Montessori spoke of: early childhood, sensitive period for protection; later childhood, moral sensitive period; adolescence, sensitive period for heroism.

The maternal type of religiousness that the Good Shepherd image arouses in younger children develops and becomes integrated as the child grows. But this development unfolds on the secure basis of the fulfillment of a fundamental need, that need Erikson termed "the need for affiliation";[10] that is, the need to be loved in a profound way. Only in the gratification of this exigence is there created that basic trust which puts us in harmony with the world. An initiation based on the Good Shepherd image thus situates the relationship with God on the foundation of "basic trust" and, translating this expression into religious terms, we speak of "trusting faith." And what else can be the foundation of the religious life?

Doctrinal Content

So great is the importance of the Good Shepherd parable that it becomes the reference point and unifying center of all the principal themes touched on in the catechesis for young children.

The child knows how to link it with the other subjects he gradually comes to know in a spontaneous synthesis that is oftentimes rich in theological content. Frequently the child connects this parable with the death and resurrection and the image of light. See the drawing (fig. 13) depicting the crucifixion, where it is written "The Good Shepherd" and "Jesus, You are risen." The light that so often emanates from the Good Shepherd is the paschal light; the illustration of the paschal candle beside the Good Shepherd also occurs frequently (fig. 14). The light surrounding the sheep, or the lighted candle beside each sheep (fig. 15), indicates that the child feels personally involved in the mystery of the resurrection. Baptism is the transmission of this light (cf. chapter 5). The sheepfold is positioned close to the Eucharistic table, as in drawing number 16 where the sheepfold is on one side and the altar is in the central position; in drawing number 17, the Shepherd who guides His sheep is placed beside the figure of Jesus, present in the Eucharist by the power of the Holy Spirit, as the one who feeds His friends (cf. also chapter 4).

Thus the parable not only satisfies the psychological needs of early childhood but it also introduces the children into the nucleus of the Christian mystery in its greatest content. In the parable, the affective and cognitive components balance one another in a wonderful way. From the doctrinal point of view, the parable is a fundamental text[11] that centers on the mystery of the person of Christ and His relationship with us, a relationship at once personal (the Shepherd knows each sheep by name) and communal (the sheepfold). It is the parable of the providential love that reaches the ultimate sacrifice of life, and as such it is a paschal parable. Christian tradition has in fact always given it a special place during the Easter season.

The child finds peace and joy in the Good Shepherd parable, for it offers him that strengthening and invigorating food he needs. We are firmly convinced that it is the greatest realities that are to be given to the youngest children. It is only in the greatest realities that the essentiality of the "metaphysical" child is fulfilled. Moreover, only if we know how to help the child center on the vital nucleus of reality will he be able, as he grows, to go ever more deeply into reality without becoming disillusioned. The parable will gradually unfold all its riches to the child, and he will integrate his childlike vision with visions that are always wider and more complete, without however having to disown anything he received previously.

NOTES

1. For the centrality of Christ in catechesis, see *Il Rinnovamento della Catechesi*, nos. 57, 58; Alberich, *op. cit.*, p. 102: "The kerygma is essentially and primarily the proclamation of Christ, and above all of the paschal mystery of his death and resurrection which establishes him in his dignity as Christ and Lord."

2. Cf. B. F. Skinner and W. Correll, *Pensare ed apprendere* (Brescia: La Scuola, 1974), p. 17: "When learning is unfolded before the student as a region that has already been explored, the opportunity to conquer personally a frontier of the unknown is taken away from him." J. Piaget, "To Understand Is to Discover, or to Reconstruct by Re-Discovery," *Education on the Move* (Paris: UNESCO Press, 1975), pp. 86–92.

3. *Gaudium et Spes* 16 (1969).

4. For the importance of the Good Shepherd parable to children who are ill, see the following by Jerome Berryman: "Discussing the Ethics of Research on Children," *Research on Children,* ed. Jan van Eys (Baltimore: University Park Press, 1978), pp. 97ff; "A Gift of Healing Stories for a Child who is Ill," *Liturgy,* Vol. 24, No. 4 (July-August, 1979), pp. 15–20, 38–42; "Being In Parables with Children," *Religious Education,* Vol. 74, No. 3 (May-June, 1979).

5. O. Dubuisson, *Le dessin au catéchisme* (Paris: Éd. du Centurion, 1968), pp. 72, 78.

6. G. Milanesi, *Psicologia della religione,* pp. 101–121.

7. R. Vianello, *La religiosità infantile* (Firenze: Giunti Barberà, 1976), pp. 195, 201, 263. Works such as Vianello's are of great use and interest, insofar as they highlight a particular situation. Nonetheless, it is necessary to be careful so as not to draw generalized conclusions from certain factual data, which could be understood in the sense of a presumed incapacity in the child. A confusion of this kind could be created not so much from Vianello's book—where the author repeatedly emphasizes the precarious and fragmentary nature of researches in general—as from his article "L'idea di Dio nel bambino," *Vita dell'infanzia* (Maggio-Giugno, 1976), pp. 9–10.

8. J. Piaget, *The Child's Conception of the World* (New Jersey: Humanities Press, 1929). French Edition, *La représentation du monde chez l'enfant* (Paris: Alcan, 1926). Italian Edition, *La rappresentazione del mondo nel fanciullo* (Torino: Boringhieri, 1974), p. 358.

9. A. Vergote, *The Religious Man* (Dublin: Macmillan, 1969). French Edition, *Psychologie Religieuse* (Bruxelles: Charles Dessart, 1966). Italian Edition, *Psicologia religiosa* (Torino: Borla, 1967), pp. 170–174.

10. E. Erikson, *Childhood and Society* (New York: Norton, 1964). Italian Edition, *Infanzia e società,* (Roma: Armando, 1967).

11. I. de la Potterie, *Gesù Verità* (Torino: Marietti, 1973), pp. 54–84: the author maintains that the Good Shepherd parable is "the synthesis of Johannine theology."

Chapter Four
Christ the Good Shepherd and the Eucharist

"You prepare a table before me."
Psalm 23:5

There are various ways in which Christ is present in the midst of mankind, yet the Eucharistic presence has a unique character.[1] Accordingly, the Eucharist should have a special position in catechesis, keeping in mind however that today there is great insistence on the unity of life, Bible, and liturgy.[2] There does not exist a Bible that we read and the Liturgy that we live; there is the Bible we live with the whole of our life and especially so in the Liturgy. The former without the latter is deprived of its most intense moment of life; the latter without the former would be based on a void. The Bible finds its fullness in the listening of the community that lives in justice and builds itself in the Eucharistic celebration. Therefore, the child who comes to know the Good Shepherd should be initiated into the greatest action in which we meet Him: the Mass. The Italian Episcopal document on catechesis states: "Catechesis constantly proposes Jesus as the living center of its very message, and manifests Jesus present and acting in the most holy Eucharist" (no. 72; cf. no. 46).

The essentiality of the child has been our invaluable guide in regard to the Eucharist. For twenty years we searched along winding paths for the best approach to the Mass for the youngest children, without success. When at last we found what seems to us to be the right road we realized that it is also the simplest and most essential: The Mass is the place and time in which we encounter our Good Shepherd in a most particular way: He calls

79

His sheep to come around His altar to feed them with Himself in a special way. It is so simple, but it took twenty years to discover!

The child's essentiality directed us to concentrate our efforts on the Eucharistic part of the Mass, that is, the part following the Liturgy of the Word. All catechesis is in some way a Liturgy of the Word, for in the parables and historical events of Jesus' life it is God's Word we are announcing to the child; we pause to meditate on the Word and respond to it with prayer. However, it is only in the Eucharist that a most particular presence of Christ is realized and it is therefore natural that the children are most involved in the Eucharistic prayer when we celebrate the Mass.

At the beginning of our endeavors, we would suggest to the children, who were more or less in the year of their first communion,* that they write their own missals. In order for the children to do so, we had at our disposal a booklet on the Mass prepared by Maria Montessori, which she entitled "The Open Book." The children would begin to transcribe, starting with the Liturgy of the Word, and they were to have finished with the communion rite; not one child ever reached the end of this work.

Recognizing this, we then began to present only the Eucharistic prayer to the children (at that time there was only the Roman canon) beginning with the consecration and concluding with the rite of communion. We saw with wonder that, by starting our presentation with the most essential moment, the children not only would copy the whole missal including the Liturgy of the Word, but it often happened that they would spontaneously write their missal as many as three times. Once more we realized that our failure did not depend on the child's incapacity nor on the difficulty of the work; it was due to the fact that we had not found the path that led through to the nucleus.

The Link between Bible and Liturgy

Our approach to the Mass with young children develops in two stages: The first is kerygmatic, the second consists in the reading of the liturgical signs.

The proclamation of the Good Shepherd's presence in our lives, which the children received through the parable, is specified at this stage in the indication of a time and a place in which

*Cavalletti is assuming an open-graded classroom with older children present in addition to those who are 3–6 years old.

the Shepherd is close to His sheep in a most particular manner and that He feeds His sheep in a most special way with His love. The Shepherd always gives His life for His sheep, but it is necessary, in our consideration, not to link this "giving His life" exclusively to the moment of death. Christ's whole life is a gift to the Father and to mankind; His death represents the ultimate concretization of His continuing gift of self offered throughout all time to all men, and comes to each one of us especially in the Eucharist. The child is perhaps more sensitive to Christ's complete availability with regard to himself, and to the awareness that Christ is constantly close to him, rather than the recognition that He committed Himself even unto death.

The bond between the Good Shepherd parable and the Eucharist is also reinforced sensorially in the material: beside the sheepfold we place another circular base covered with a green cloth, almost carpetlike in texture, which by its color is reminiscent of a pasture; on the other circular base we put a miniature altar with a small statue of the Good Shepherd placed on top. Then we say to the children: "The Good Shepherd calls each of His sheep by name to come close to Him around His altar and one by one the sheep assemble around the altar. Now they are near to Him once again, in another sheepfold which we call the 'church,' a fold where we too go when Mass is celebrated. Here the Good Shepherd's presence has a totally special character. He is really there for me, to give Himself completely to me. The Shepherd's presence is not tied to the little wooden statue; this is only a way to help us think of Him. At Mass the Good Shepherd is present in the signs of the bread and wine. (At this point we place the models of the chalice and paten on the altar.) We can even take away the tall statue (we remove the Good Shepherd figure from the altar); it does not change anything with regard to the life-giving presence of our Shepherd." The spellbound silence—which is prayer without words—that accompanies the children's contemplation of the sheep around the altar often becomes an explicit prayer of thanksgiving.

This is the first phase of our presentation, the purpose of which is to allow the children to see the sheep around the altar, thus establishing the bond between the biblical dimension (Good Shepherd parable) and the liturgical dimension (the Mass) in a visible way. At this point we do not intend to enter into a discussion as to *how* the Eucharistic presence is realized, but rather to renew the proclamation that the Good Shepherd "remains" in us and we in Him in the Eucharist in an altogether special way. The proclamation of the Eucharistic presence will be resumed later and integrated through the narration of the Last Supper (cf. chapter 6).

It is necessary to prolong this first phase of the kerygmatic presentation until the children have internalized the image of the sheep around the altar. Then follows the second phase: It is the moment when each sheep is a small wooden figure of a person; therefore at this point the children should have already discovered that the sheep are people. We say to the children: "Among these persons there is one who has a special mission; he is called the priest. His mission is to repeat the words of Jesus, to express His will to 'remain' with men of all times."

At this point the material portrays the image of what the child sees at Mass: "the real fold" (the church) and "the false fold," as one boy said, are a unity in the child's mind. So complete is this unity that Stefania (five years old), with a wonderful intuition, illustrated the altar table as a meadow (fig. 22). Maurizio (six years old) expressed the same concept in drawing sheep and people together around the altar (fig. 19). Doriano (six years old) enclosed the Shepherd, sheep, and altar within the one circle, which recalls the sheepfold (fig. 20). It is remarkable that the altar is often depicted as round in form (figs. 18, 21) even though, both in the material and in reality, the altar is rectangular. Roberta (five years old) actually made the altar a part of Christ's body, to which are attached the faces of the faithful (fig. 24), although she had never heard of the Pauline image of the body and its members.

In our view, it is very important to help the children reach the synthesis between the parable and the liturgical moment, both for the objective reasons we have stated and also because in this way the Eucharistic celebration is charged with the whole conceptual and affective potential of the parable. The greater the resonance the parable has within the child, the richer and more profound will be the resonance of the Eucharist within him.

The Eucharist as the "Sacrament of the Gift"

The first presentation is a way, it seems to us, in which an important dimension of the Mass is revealed. The children are nevertheless capable of going farther and entering more deeply into its significance, or at least into one of its many aspects. The

Mass is a very rich reality; the adult's problem is to find the aspect that corresponds to the child's capacity and fulfills his needs. The aspect relating to the needs of the adolescent, who is oriented toward the ideal of the *imitatio Christi,* may be the dimension of his own personal participation in the Mass through his own self-offering. But what is the aspect for the young child? Research has not been easy and our failures induced us to think for a number of years that the Mass was too great a reality for the child, that it would be necessary to wait until a more mature age for a serious introduction to the Eucharist. Actually our failure, we should reiterate, was due to the fact that we had not found the right path.

The aspect of the Mass that has been demonstrated to respond to the young child's capacities is that of the "sacrament of the gift." That is, the Mass is presented as the most particular concretization of that continuous gift the Father sends us in the person of His Son, incarnate, dead and risen, and of the gift with which man endeavors to respond to the Father. The Mass is this wonderful exchange of gifts between heaven and earth; or, better, it is the culmination of the many gifts the Father gives to mankind and the culmination of the many ways in which man tries to respond as fully as possible to the gift received.

The means we use to present the Mass as the sacrament of the gift are two gestures. In the first stage of our presentation, the children listened to the renewed proclamation of the Good Shepherd's presence in their lives, whereas in this second stage the children are called to read the language of signs. This is not the time to pause and discuss the efficacy and immediacy of the language of gestures.[3] It is primarily a visual language; as such it is especially suited to children for whom verbal language may still offer some difficulties. We know how children are interested in everything involving movement. Also, linking our presentation to gestures the children will see during Mass provides us with a way of starting a direct initiation into the liturgical celebration. The children find in these gestures a reference point that acts as an immediate aid to their conscious participation in the celebration.

The first of the two gestures is the imposition of the hands (or *cheirotonia*) accompanying the prayer of invocation to the Father to send the Holy Spirit to transform the bread and wine. The second is the gesture of offering concluding the Eucharistic prayer, when the priest raises the consecrated bread and wine together to offer them to the Father with the prayer "Through Him, with Him, in Him." These are two complementary gestures that express in an evident manner the gift that comes from above at the divine initiative, and the response offered from earth to heaven. They result in a global and essential presentation of the reality of the Mass; they are an efficacious and immediate means of initiating children to a fundamental point of biblical theology: the theology of the covenant. As with all the other themes, this presentation should be developed and integrated later on; however, its content is such that it forms the basis for the successive approaches to the Mass. The younger child will delight especially in the contemplation of the gift the Father gives him; the older child, who is in the moral sensitive period, will place the accent on the hands that are raised from earth to heaven and on the commitment that assures they are not offered in an empty gesture; the adolescent will begin to open himself to the reality of his relationship with God, which consists in an exchange of love that involves him wholly.

The presentation develops in two phases. The first concerns the imposition of the hands. In the line of the Eastern Orthodox tradition, contemporary theology stresses the transformative action of the Holy Spirit in the Eucharistic consecration, and hence the importance of the prayer of epiclesis and the gesture accompanying it: the imposition of the hands.[4] The gesture, one could say, is a "visible prayer": it expresses in a visual way what the words are saying:

And so, Father, we bring you these gifts.
We ask you to make them holy by the power of your Spirit,
that they may become the body and blood
of your Son, our Lord Jesus Christ,
at whose command we celebrate this eucharist.
                              (Eucharistic Prayer III, Latin Liturgy)[5]

We should assist the children to probe the meaning of this first phase through the gesture; we should let the gesture speak as much as possible. As we said, gestures speak an extremely effective language, which we should be careful not to stultify with too many words. The child's attention should focus on the gesture more than on what we are saying.

For the first presentation, a table is prepared with a cloth covering and the models of a chalice and paten (*not* a real chalice and paten). The catechist recalls the gesture the children may have already seen the priest do at Mass. Then, in silence and with great solemnity, the catechist stands and enacts the gesture of the imposition of the hands over the two models. Afterward, the catechist is seated again and begins to meditate with the children on the meaning of what has been shown them: "What does this gesture make us think of? Maybe it makes us think of someone who wants to give us something? Of a gift that comes from where? From above? And then from whom? The Father gives us so many gifts, but in this moment of the Mass what special gift do we ask of Him?" We have described how a four-year-old girl went immediately to the essential of this action and explained that the priest "calls the Holy Spirit into the bread and wine." Before passing to the second phase, we should give the children the necessary space to interiorize the first part of the presentation, allowing them the time to do the gesture by themselves and to say the accompanying prayer as many times as they wish.

Then we begin the second phase. We prepare the table and models as before and recall the gesture of the imposition of the hands; then we do the gesture of offering with great solemnity. Once again we reflect on its significance with the children: "This time the palms are turned upward. It is the reverse of the gesture of the epiclesis. What does this mean? The hands turned upward make us 'see' the gift the Father sends us. But when we receive something that makes us happy, what do we do? Maybe we want to show in some way that we are thankful and happy? Maybe we want to try to offer something ourselves? If we are really so happy, perhaps we look for the most precious thing we have. Let's listen to the words the priest prays while he lifts up the consecrated bread and wine:

> Through him,
> with him,
> in him,
> in the unity of the Holy Spirit,
> all glory and honor is yours,
> almighty Father,
> for ever and ever.

"The priest makes the gestures and prays the words, but we are not there only to stand and watch. We too want to express our joy in receiving the gift and to show that this gesture of offerings is ours as well, so we respond in a loud voice: 'Amen.' Or maybe we sing it many times, because it is the most important Amen we pray in the Mass."

The Theological Aspect

The phrase "sacrament of the gift" we propose is certainly not a common expression; however, it is quite close to the term used by some theologians who speak of the "sacramental sacrifice" or of the "sacrament of the sacrifice of Christ."[6] The difference between sacrament of the gift and sacrament of the sacrifice is in the different accentuation given to the same reality. Both expressions signify "offering," but "sacrifice" stresses the painful dimension every offering involves, whereas "gift" emphasizes the gratifying aspect that is no less present in every offering that has love as its origin.

The theological richness of the theme of gift is great, although it is hardly taken into consideration. It is an element of primary importance in the Gospel of Saint John; it has been observed that "the theme of the gift is used by John to express the whole theology of the Word incarnate in its three principal aspects: the mission, the person, the saving activity. Everything is gift in the history of salvation worked by God, through Christ and in Christ."[7]

Therefore, in speaking of the sacrament of the gift, we do not risk diminishing the reality of the Eucharist, even if we focus especially on one aspect, that is, gratification. It is a dimension that nevertheless can be easily integrated with a commitment to effort and even suffering, when the child's age allows (figs. 8, 23). Indeed, not every age can receive every aspect of the Christian reality and, in our estimation, early childhood is the time of the serene enjoyment of God. We have already mentioned the aspect of enjoyment in the religious fact; we believe it is afforded too little attention in general, and particularly in relation to the religious initiation of children.

The Element of Enjoyment in the Relationship with God

Psychology places strong emphasis on the importance that an experience of prereligious happiness may have in the relationship with God. We ask ourselves whether the experience of happiness must necessarily be sought apart from and prior to the religious experience, or, rather, if the accent could not be shifted to the relationship with God itself, especially in early childhood. We remember the special quality of enchantment the child shows when he is spoken to of God, his capacity to be pensive and recollected for long periods of time while he ponders within himself the proclamation he has received, as if he wanted to absorb to the fullest an element essential for his life. We recall the state of deep and tranquil peace these moments of recollection create in the child.

Too often we obscure or actually impede this enjoyment with preoccupations—especially those that are moralistic in character, with normative superstructures that take away the spontaneity and enchantment from the encounter with God. If we put too great or too early an emphasis on man's response, our attention will be centered on man rather than on God and then strain will prevail in our relationship with God. If we become too preoccupied with what we ourselves must do, then it becomes impossible for us to stop and enjoy God's initiative, and thus we will ruin the relationship of covenant.

It is obvious that moral education and also a certain kind of preparation for struggle and sacrifice are necessary. But there is "a time for everything," as Ecclesiastes says, and early childhood is not the time for moral effort. In our view, early childhood is a period of tranquil growth when the child, still free from cares of any kind, can give himself completely—and does give himself if the conditions permit him—to the enjoyment of the persons and things he has been given. After the age of six other factors come into consideration, and the child's horizon will no longer be so clear. The time for accentuating man's work will come, the time for the invitation to moral commitment on the behavioral plane will come; but we must not anticipate or confuse the times. If we do, we preclude the child's access to that aspect of God the child most needs. In our estimation, we compromise the child's very moral formation, which should be based on love, and should be the response of the child's love to the love that God first gave him. We confuse, as we will say later, the face of God Himself.

Our highlighting even the aspect of offering with young children could appear to be a contradiction to what was said earlier. The nuance is subtle, yet real and important: Offering something to the giver of a gift is a spontaneous gesture when the child is very happy; in such an instance, offering is an expression of joy. After focusing on the aspect of "gift," and allowing the children all the time they need to contemplate and enjoy it, spontaneously there is generated within the child a desire to express in some way the enchantment he experiences. The hands that are lifted up are a manifestation of the child's joy and not as yet of his moral commitment. They are offering, not sacrificing: Sacrifice, as we said, requires effort and pain; offering flows spontaneously from a joyful heart.

In fact, the children's reaction to the presentation of the Mass as the sacrament of the gift was immediate and profound; they seemed to be there as if awaiting something of this kind. The children appropriated this aspect of the Eucharist with surprising readiness; it took root in them in a spontaneous, simple, and profound manner. They continued to refer to it during their discussions and reflections as they would to something they had always known.

The Responsiveness of the Children

To illustrate how the work described up to this point resounds in the children, and in adults as well, we include an excerpt from the diary of a group of catechists in Our Lady of Lourdes parish (Tormarancia, Rome):

December 11, 1974, a group of children from four to six years of age.

The children knew the Bishop would be coming on a pastoral visit to meet them. However their work was organized as usual; when the Bishop came in some children were working with the large green base of the sheepfold and the other circular base with the prepared altar table on it. They were taking the sheep from the fold and putting them around the altar, on which the Good Shepherd, chalice and paten were placed. A catechist accompanied the Bishop to the table. Gradually all the other children also came over and we were all together.

The Bishop declines the chair and sits on the small stool among the children. Some children are responding to the catechist's questions, others are speaking among themselves or with the Bishop. They are saying we are the sheep, that the Good Shepherd takes us to places where "we are happy," that the Shepherd wants to meet us especially at Mass, when "He comes just to be with us." One child moves his hands in the gesture of the epiclesis, and another child says: "Let's put away the Good Shepherd statue; there's the bread and wine. It is the same."

The Bishop seems to be holding his breath; then he asks: "Who is it that makes the gesture [of the imposition of the hands]?" The children reply: "The priest." "And who is the priest?" the Bishop asks. Fabrizio answers: "A special sheep who says the words and does the gesture." Marco, pointing to the Bishop, says: "You!"

One of us asks: "The Father gave us Jesus. What can we give him?" Earlier in the year the children had drawn and cut out two hands with the palms facing upward. At this moment they go to get the hands and begin to place what represents their object of offering on them: the Good Shepherd, many put a sheep there, others bring a wooden figure of a person to show their own personal sharing in the offering. Each of the catechists places a sheep in the hands as well. Everyone has brought something, except the Bishop. Then there is a moment of deep silence and waiting. Finally Giulia turns to the Bishop and says: "And your sheep?" The Bishop, visibly moved, takes a sheep, puts it in the palms of the cut out hands, saying: "If I am worthy to."

A little while later the Bishop commented on what he had seen; still deeply moved he said: "I had a big shock. I will never be able to talk about the Good Shepherd as I did before." He said that from now on he would speak of the Shepherd as "a unique figure of union and love." The Bishop also remarked on the "communion" he felt here. What impressed him most was that such young children could speak about such great things in so natural, profound and serious a way.

The Affective Impact of the Theme of "Gift"

We ask ourselves if the theme of gift does not touch a chord within the innermost depths of the child. F. Fornari observes:

The maternal factor, in its modality of encounter with the child, radically decides man's whole life, inasmuch as it transcends the biological datum on which it is founded, in order to acquire the significance of a "gift" *the presence of which is indispensable and sufficient to create a basic gratification of the "I", and the absence of which impedes that "I" from establishing itself, and exposes it to more or less serious disasters.*

(Fornari's *emphasis*)

He continues to say that this affirmation, "shared by the majority of scholars as well, has a distinctly mystical flavour. Such an affirmation in fact may summon in a surprising way the religious question of grace . . . ."[8]

A gift is a positive experience at any age, yet there is an age when it can become constitutive of the person. The gift of the mother's presence, based on the most recent psychological research, is essential to and exceedingly gratifying for the child. It deals with a relationship that "transcends the biological datum," as Fornari observes; that is, it not only offers the physical well-being of warmth and food but it also unites mother and child in a true affective relationship. And the child needs this more than food; this is a well-known fact, which we have mentioned. We wonder what influence it could have on a child who is placed in the condition of becoming gradually conscious of a gift such as God's presence, a gift that is unfailing and surpasses the limits proper to every human relationship. We ask ourselves if, by presenting the Mass in the way we outlined, we do not situate the foundational experience of gift on a more solid base than that of maternal love, which is of course human and thus limited. In any event, we touch that same profound chord which is sounded by the Good Shepherd parable. The sacrament of the gift and the Good Shepherd parable relate to and integrate one another reciprocally, fusing Bible and Liturgy in a nourishing synthesis. The gratifying experience they both offer contributes, in our estimation, to placing the child in harmony with the world and to basing his relationship with God on the essential foundation of trusting faith.

Introductory Work on the Mass

In relation to the work we do with the children on the Mass, what we have described up to this point is the richest in content. However, it is preceded by a number of exercises involving nomenclature and movement that, although poor in meaning, are nevertheless quite useful to the children and prepare the way for more complex work. The character of this work is sensorial and therefore responds to the child's needs. The children, using small models of the altar and the articles and priest's vestments associated with the Mass, learn their names and function by means of the three-period lesson. In the first part of the lesson the catechist indicates the object and says its name, for example, "This is the chalice"; in the second part the catechist says only the name and asks the child to identify the object, "Where is the chalice?"; in the last part it is the child who names the object in response to the catechist's question, "What is this?"

The altar is first presented as a table, which the catechist prepares in a special way saying: "On the altar there is an altar cloth, a beautiful cup called the chalice, and a beautiful plate called the paten." The children will find these elements in the successive work on the Mass. Also on the altar are the lighted candles and the cross, symbols of the resurrection.

It is only in the second presentation that we show the children the model of the lectern with the book of God's Word; thus, even at this introductory level, we focus primarily on the Eucharistic part of the Mass. These presentations concern elementary knowledge, but they too are important in that, by providing vocabulary, they offer the children the opportunity of developing a work that is richer in content later on. Numerous mothers remark that as their children come to know these things their attitude to Mass changes. Church is no longer a place where everything is unknown to them; now they see objects that are familiar, even if they are larger and more beautiful than the models with which the children work.

As to the dimensions of the altar, we think it best that the altar table be much smaller than an average child-sized table. The models of the articles and priest's vestments associated with the Mass should also be considerably smaller than their regular dimensions. In this way it is clearer to the children that these are materials for exercises only.

There is additional introductory work intended to teach the children those things that they can do themselves when participating at Mass. This work could serve as the younger children's preparation immediately before Mass, during the time when the community of older children and adults is also preparing by meditating on the Scripture readings for Mass. This preparatory work is comprised of elementary exercises: The children learn to

fill the normal-sized cruets, to pour the water for the washing of
the hands, and to prepare the chalice with wine and a few drops
of water as the priest does at the altar.

According to an allegorical explanation, the drops of water
poured in the chalice represent man and the wine represents
Christ. Even if there is a current tendency to eliminate symbolism of this kind, we continue to present it for the particular response such symbolism elicits in the children. This exercise is
generally done by the youngest children; yet we will never forget
seven-year-old Massimo, who continued to repeat this exercise
for so long a period of time. The catechist, thinking that he was
doing it out of laziness, came up to him several times to introduce him to some other work; but Massimo's facial expression
was intent and rapt and he was trying to explain the meaning of
what he was doing as he repeated the various actions; what he
was saying, however, was unclear. The catechist observed his return time and time again to this activity, always with the same
concentration, and she let him continue to do it. Finally—it was
almost the end of the year—he managed to say: "A few drops of
water and a lot of wine, because we must lose ourselves in Jesus." For the entire year the child, through the very simple details of that exercise, had been considering the mysterious union
of Christ with mankind. In the end Massimo had known how to
express it with words worthy of a mystic.

The work on the Mass continues naturally in the second cycle, the period during which the child celebrates first communion. In the second cycle we concentrate primarily on another
fundamental moment of the Mass, the communion, by focusing
once more on the gestures: the breaking of the bread, and the exchange of "peace." As we mentioned earlier, the moment of offering, which the children already know, now begins to assume a
moral dimension.

To recapitulate briefly, the work of the Mass pivots on three
points: the Eucharistic presence, the offering, and for the older
children, the communion; all three are linked to a gesture that
renders its presentation more impressive. We apply here, as in
all the other major themes, the Montessori principle of "isolating
the difficulties." In the area of religion this principle becomes
"isolate the points of greatest theological content." The method
of the "spiral" can be applied to all the main points we highlight;
that is, the approach of a progressive deepening that orients the
younger and older child, and adult as well, toward the unfathom-

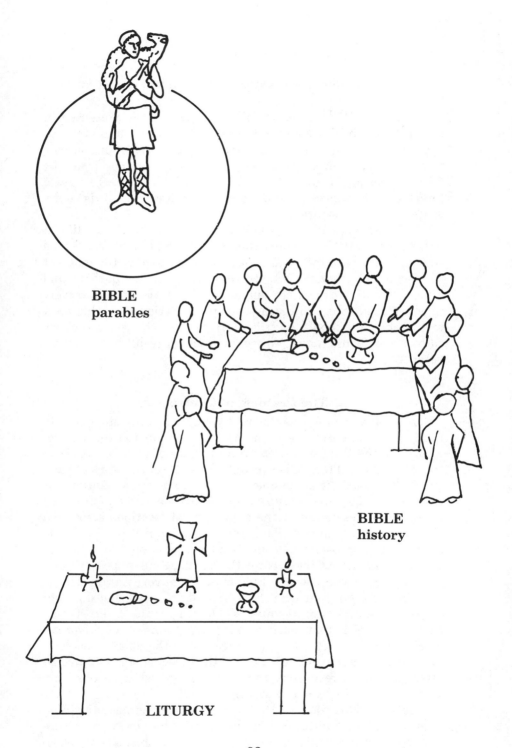

BIBLE
parables

BIBLE
history

LITURGY

ability of the reality one is entering. But we will say more about this later.

Even with the youngest children, the Mass is presented in various ways, beginning with the sensorial approach (altar, articles, priest's vestments) and advancing to the area of deeper content. The work directly related to the Mass unfolds from the biblical—parabolic and historical (about which more will be said later)—and liturgical points of view. This development is represented in the illustration.

All this work has a long-range effect on the child's life; it will be seen only later when the older child becomes concerned that his hands are raised in a significant gesture at the moment of offering. On this subject, see the drawings that Barbara and Simone did when they were ten and eleven years old respectively (figs. 8, 23). For the adult's part, our presentation of all this work to the children should be "disinterested" in the sense that we cannot and should not try to see its practical result in the child's behavior.

The Problem of Controls

A work as complex as this really poses the problem of how to verify what we ourselves are doing. Is it possible to exert control over what the children receive from themes of such far-reaching scope? In general terms, is it possible to control the work of catechesis? Obviously it is possible and easy to do so in relation, for example, to the nomenclature of the articles and vestments used at Mass, or the names of the geographical locations associated with Jesus in the land of Palestine. However, is it possible to do so when we approach the level of profound content?

We believe that the greater the theme, the less possible and justified it is to exercise any kind of action of verification. This is especially true in that what we transmit is a seed that does not belong to us, and even less may we claim its fruits. Saint Augustine, who was a great teacher, said: "*Ego numquam possum docere*" (I can never teach).[9] In the presence of the Spirit who blows "wherever he wills and as he wills," the catechist should have an attitude of deep reverence and gratitude for what he has been given to see, yet without expecting to see.

So it is with courage that we renounce asking unjustified questions of the child. I say "with courage" because certain controls that are academic in nature give the catechist a sense of security, which is nonetheless empty: The catechist teaches, the child appears to know, and the adult has a quiet conscience. But this may be done on a scholastic, not a catechetical level. When speaking of matters of profound spiritual significance, all controls become illusory; we cannot exercise such control even on ourselves. Who among us knows how conscious he is of God's presence in his own life? Who among us knows to what extent he lets himself become involved in the Eucharistic action?

The catechist who seeks security in academic controls is looking for security in the wrong place. Are we really sure that our work is done well when the child answers all our questions? Very often too prompt a reply may be the sign that what has been communicated has stayed on the surface, that the child has repeated mechanically what he has heard without any personal participation. A personal response is to be sought within the depths of oneself; this requires time. On the crest of the wave there may be resplendent colors, but what matters is what is happening in the currents below. And there we cannot and should not enter.

The catechist who looks for security precludes, we think, the possibility of the greatest joy, the joy of feeling sometimes, in the work that unfolds, the passing of a force we clearly perceive is not our own, an imperceptible breath that lets us know that it is not us but the Spirit who works within hearts. What is exultant about these moments is precisely the fact that it is something that is *not* of our doing, something that is far greater than we and totally exceeds what we could have given. It is the mustard seed beginning to sprout; yet the mysterious wonder of this growth is that it happens "of itself," while the sower "knows not how." These are moments when the presence of God is tangible, though the catechist will be able to relish them only if she knows how to repeat the words of Sion:

> Who has borne me these?
> I was childless and barren,
> who has brought these up?
> I was left all alone,
> and now, where do these come from?
>   (Isaiah 49:21)

It is this very comparison between our sterility and the fecundity of the Word within the child that fills us with a joy without words.

At times we may find an indication of our work: in some unexpected response from the children, in some work they have done; perhaps, more than all else, in their attitude of recollection and serene joy; or in the prayer flowing spontaneously from each theme that has touched the child in the depths of his person. Nevertheless, we are dealing with manifestations that occur when we least expect them; these should be accepted as a gift, not claimed as a right.

The catechist's only security comes from faith: in God and His creature, in God Who speaks to His creatures. It is necessary to relinquish all other forms of security, in the spirit of poverty. Poverty is, I believe, the fundamental virtue of the catechist.

NOTES

1. This is emphasized in numerous documents of the Second Vatican Council. See also C. Vagaggini, *Theological Dimensions of the Liturgy,* trans. Leonard J. Doyle (Collegeville, Minnesota: Liturgical Press, 1959). Italian Edition, *Il senso teologico della Liturgia* (Roma: EP, 1965), pp. 329, 464, 177–180, et passim.

2. T. Federici, *Bibbia e Liturgia* (Roma: Pontificio Istituto Liturgico, 1973–1975) (MS).

3. A. Vergote, "Symbolic Gestures and Actions in the Liturgy," *Concilium* 62 (1971), pp. 40–52. Italian edition, A. Vergote, "Gesti e azioni simboliche nella liturgia," *Concilium* (1971), pp. 55–70. We draw your attention to the importance given to the epiclesis in the Eucharistic prayers for children composed by P. Borobio and V. ma. Pedrosa, *Celebración de la Eucarestía con los niños* (Phase, 1972), pp. 9–76; note in particular the link between Pentecost and the epiclesis, which emphasizes the continuing work of the Spirit.

4. See *Ephemerides Liturgicae,* Nos. 3–4 and 5–6 (1976), both of which are dedicated to this topic, and in particular J. H. McKenna, "The Eucharistic Epiclesis in the Twentieth Century Theology," pp. 289–328, 446–482. McKenna is writing a book on the same theme to be published by Alcuin Club.

5. Other shorter forms can be found in *La Messa dei fanciulli* (Libreria Editrice Vaticana, 1976). English editions: *Directory for Masses with Children* (1973), U.S. Catholic Conference; *Eucharistic Prayers for Masses with Children and for Masses of*

Reconciliation, Provisional text (Bishop's Committee on the Liturgy, Washington, D.C. 1975).

6. C. Vagaggini, "La Messa sacramento del sacrificio pasquale di Cristo e della Chiesa," *Rivista Liturgica* (1969), pp. 179–209; S. Marsili, "Verso una nuova teologia eucaristica," *Via, Verità e Vita,* 22 (1969), pp. 15, 13–28, and "Forma e contenuto nella preghiera eucaristica," *Rivista di Pastorale Liturgica* (1973), pp. 204–220.

7. O. Battaglia, *La teologia del dono* (Assisi: Cittadella, 1971), p. 251. See also the article on gift by M. Mauss in *Temi generali della magia* (Torino: Einaudi, 1965).

8. F. Fornari, *La vita affettiva originaria del bambino* (Milano: Feltrinelli, 1971), p. 230. Also E. Fromm, *The Anatomy of Human Destructiveness* (New York: Holt, Rinehart & Winston, 1973). Italian Edition, *Anatomia della distruttivita unama* (Milano: Mondadori, 1975), p. 452: Fromm, speaking of the mother's love, writes: "Her love is grace."

9. St. Augustine, *De Magistro,* XIV, 45.

Chapter Five
Christ the Light and Baptism

"The light shines in the darkness."
John 1:5

For every subject we present to the children we need what we might call "the linking point," that is, an especially striking element that emphasizes the vital nucleus of the theme. The linking point should introduce us into the heart of the subject in such a way that it gives us, in a flash, the global intuition of the essence of the subject we are considering. It is a cognitive instrument that is applied first to the intuition, the validity of which is then successively evaluated in the light of a more specifically rational process. The linking point should be rich in meaning, so that in our continual reference to it, it will help us to go always more deeply into the theme. The subject presented is contained in the linking point as a tree is contained in the seed, in a way that it is capable of opening to us an ever greater and deeper knowledge. It is evident that we should look for the linking point among the "signs." It is not necessarily the most important liturgical or theological element; in Baptism, for instance, the linking point is the light.

Light has an immediate effect on the sense and it is psychologically gratifying and reassuring; thus the child associates the image of Christ the Light with the Good Shepherd and consequently the effect of the former image is reinforced. Furthermore, it is well known what importance the image of Christ-Light has had, especially in relation to Baptism, in the entire Christian tradition beginning with Saint Paul and the Church Fathers[1] up to our present understanding of Liturgy.

Saint Paul speaks of Baptism as our participation in the death and resurrection of Christ:

> When we were baptized we went into the tomb with him and joined him in death, so that as Christ was raised from the dead by the Father's glory, we too might live a new life. If in union with Christ we have imitated his death, we shall also imitate him in his resurrection.
>
> (Romans 6:4–5)

Obviously we cannot speak in this way to a child. Indeed, I think language such as this is difficult for many adults as well. But in Paul's writings, this presentation is associated with Baptism as "illumination":

> Awake, O sleeper,
> and arise from the dead,
> and Christ shall give you light.
>
> (Ephesians 5:14)

The catechumens are called the "enlightened" in the Letter to the Hebrews (6:4, 10:32). This is simply another way of saying the same thing: the darkness-light contrast corresponds to the passage from death to life.

We live theology in the Liturgy, and the baptismal signs let us participate in the death and resurrection of Christ by making us "see" this reality through the darkness-light contrast. The baptismal material the children work with consists of the liturgical signs of the sacrament, which are highlighted one at a time; in fact, the material contains nothing apart from these signs.

The Reading of the Baptismal Signs

When we begin our first presentation of baptism with the children, they already know about the prophecy of the Messiah-Light in Isaiah, and the Easter Liturgy of Light (see chapter 6). Therefore we link our presentation of Baptism to these elements, concretizing this linkage around the sign of the paschal candle. We initiate our narration with the image of light: "There was a long time of waiting for the light to be kindled. When Jesus was born, the light began to illumine the world. (At this point we light the paschal candle before the children's amazed faces.) However, the darkness overwhelmed the light for a moment. Jesus knew this could happen; in fact, he had said: 'The Good Shepherd gives his life for his sheep.' (Now we extinguish the candle.) But the victory of the darkness over the light was only momentary; for the light was relit, never to go out again. (We relight the paschal candle and begin to meditate with the children on this new light that illumines the world.) This is a very special light, so strong, so powerful, that never again will it be overpowered; and even more, it is a far-reaching light. The risen Christ did not want to keep this new light for Himself alone. He gives it as a gift to all those who come close to Him. From that day when the light was relit in the world, how many have received it into their hearts! How much more brightly it shines! And then one day this light came to me too, and to you. (At this moment the children are called by name one at a time to come to the paschal candle to light their own little candles.)"

Now the meditation continues on the gift of light: "How beautiful it is to have our own candle shining so brightly, and to know that on the day of our baptism a very special light was enkindled in our hearts. What a precious gift! Could we have lighted our little candles if the paschal candle had not first overpowered the darkness? Could we have this light in our hearts if Christ had not first given it to us?" Francesca (three and a half years old) explained: "Jesus gives us a loving hand so we can rise up."

In this first presentation we also show the baptismal gown to the children with words like: "This gown is so white! It is completely white! On our baptismal day, our gown covered us completely to show, even on the outside, the light we had received in our hearts; to show, even on the outside, that inside we are totally different." A catechist once asked the children: "Why are we given a white gown at our baptism?" A five-year-old girl replied: "Because the light is inside and outside us."

Then, in the second presentation, we speak of the book of God's Word and the water. Some of the points we mention are: "The light also came to us through this book and this is the way we became sheep who have the light in our hearts. The light came to us especially through that Word which makes us know God. The Gospel is the book where the secrets of God are kept, those secrets that He wants everyone to know. There is one secret you have already begun to know: that the Lord Jesus is our

Good Shepherd, and He knows all his sheep by their names. He guides them, gives them food and drink, and washes them. And God's light also came to us through the water. Water always cleans and makes life possible. But this water is given to us in the name of the Father, and of the Son, and of the Holy Spirit. It takes all the darkness away from us and we are born into the Kingdom of God 'of infinite light.' " At this point the catechist pours the water; the children hear the gentle sound of water while the catechist says the words: "I baptize you . . ." Then the children, each in their turn, pour the water and say the sacramental words.

Finally, we dedicate the third presentation to the other gestures of the baptismal rite: the imposition of the hands and the sign of the cross. As to the first gesture, we refer to the imposition of the hands, which was previously presented in relation to the Mass. Drawing number 32 is another confirmation that the children do not stay tied to the material aspect of the signs; rather, they interpret them in depth. In this drawing it is the Holy Spirit Who dominates the scene. As to the gesture of the sign of the cross, if it has not yet been presented to the children we do so now solemnly. We explain: "This is the sign of the Good Shepherd's victory over the powers of darkness. It was signed on our forehead with the thumb, as if the priest wanted to impress it within us. In fact this sign was made not just on our skin where it could be rubbed off or spoiled, but it was enclosed within our hearts, 'like the pearl of great value' (figs. 49, 50), 'like the mustard seed.' The cross was then signed over all those who were present, this time in a great gesture so that the cross could cover us all." (The catechist does this gesture in an emphatic manner.) At this point the children have often remarked, in observing the sign, "It is like a shield." Thus they re-echo, without knowing it, an image frequently found in the Psalms and the Church Fathers. Later on the children will link the baptismal sign of the cross with the one accompanying the absolution in the sacrament of reconciliation with God. At that time the "shield" will acquire a clearer meaning of defense in the struggle against evil.

The Responsiveness in the Children

As we said earlier, children have a great facility to go beyond what appears in the sign. Once, during a meditation on light with the children, a catechist was reflecting aloud on the question: "To what could we compare the baptismal light? Is it like the light of a lamp?" "Not at all," the children replied. "Is it like the light of the sun?" Francesco (six years old) responded: "No, the sun's light is a natural thing and the light of baptism is . . ." He lacked the word for "supernatural," but the difference of level was most clear to him.

Numerous prayers bear witness to the hold that the image of light has on children. Captivated with the gift they have received, they constantly give thanks to God for it (see chapter 7). This light image reappears later on in the children in reference to some moral themes we present. This fact therefore demonstrates that the enchantment they experience before the age of six is not fruitless, but rather it flowers forth and affects behavior during later childhood. This reappearance of the light image enables us to see that the "falling in love" the image calls forth has come to constitute the reactivator of the child's moral life (see chapter 9).

If we synthesize the doctrinal points the children perceive through the baptismal signs it will be seen that they contain the fundamental doctrine of Baptism. The children "see" Baptism as the *participation in the death and resurrection of Christ* through the candle that was lighted, extinguished, and relit, whose light has been communicated to us. *Becoming children of God* is perceived through the light that is transmitted to us. The *Trinitarian* presentation is aligned with the *Christocentric,* especially in the sacramental words; the Holy Spirit's action is focused on particularly in the gesture of the imposition of the hands. The *gift of God* or "grace" is also "seen" in the sign of light. The *Church is the sheepfold* where we are welcomed, loved, and protected, where all the sheep have the light and where "everyone becomes good," as one child said.

All this would be terribly laborious for the child if the liturgical elements of the sacrament did not offer us a concrete theology. It would be difficult to avoid abstractionism if the signs did not render baptismal theology so visible and tangible. As we have already said in regard to the Mass, we should be careful not to overwhelm the immediate efficacy of the language of signs with our own words. We should provide long intervals of silence during the process of presentation so as to give the child a way in which to "see" the sacrament, and what Christ is working within us and with us through it. The drawings on Baptism also show the child's unsuspected ability to synthesize. The combinations that can be noticed in many drawings are spontaneously generated in the child's mind, whereas the catechists restricted themselves to presenting one element at a time *without* making any link between them. The connections that can be seen in the children's work are the fruit of their own personal elaborations.

The images of Christ the Light and Christ the Good Shepherd often fuse together into a marvelous synthesis. See Christ the Shepherd resplendent with light in drawing number 11. A four-and-a-half year old boy traced the figure of the Good Shepherd and then pasted the paschal candle beside it (fig. 25). However, Christ is never separated from his faithful ones; the light in Rita Maria's drawing signifies the fraternal bond uniting the Shepherd and His sheep, which she described as "sheep of light" (five and a half years old; fig. 26; cf. fig. 27).

Easter is represented, in drawing number 31, in its dimensions of death (black cross) and resurrection (light around Christ) and Christ's sacramental presence (children holding candles). These three elements reappear in the drawing of Roberto (six years old): Death is indicated with the color red, the resurrection with yellow, which is also the color of the paschal candle and the sheep that goes to light its candle from it (fig. 29). The connection between the paschal mystery and baptism seems to be present to the children no less than it was to Saint Paul. A five-year-old girl had drawn a sheep following the presentation of the Good Shepherd parable. Some months later, after the presentation of Baptism, she took out her drawing once again and added a lighted candle beside the sheep, and explained: "It has the light of Jesus inside; it's not a sheep like the others, it's in His sheepfold." Marco (six years old) drew two candles beside a sheep, saying: "It is very happy"; when the catechist asked him why, Marco replied: "It is with God" (fig. 15).

Carola (six years old) joined together the sheepfold and the baptismal symbols of the white gown, light, oils, and God's Word; the sheep (only the head is drawn) goes to take the light directly from the paschal candle (fig. 28). On the same subject, the drawing of Carlo (six years old) is worthy of note: He has depicted his "becoming a sheep of Jesus" as united to Baptism with the Eucharist as the point of arrival (fig. 34).

In drawing number 49, baptism is interpreted as the "pearl of great value" and is drawn in relation to the "grown grain of wheat." In drawing number 50, the "precious stone," hidden in the heart glowing with light, is the gift of the Holy Spirit as indicated by the imposition of the hand. The children show how they move with ease in the vast field that has been opened up before them by creating combinations that are often revelatory to the adult not only of the young child's capacities but of the mysteries of God as well.

NOTES

1. Among others, see St. Gregory of Nazianzen, *Sermon* 40 (PG 36, 359 ff); in Judaeo-Christian liturgy see E. Testa, "Le origini delle tradizioni dei luoghi santi in Palestina," *Studi Biblici Francescani,* Liber Annuus XIV (1963–1964), pp. 119ff.

Chapter Six

The Historical Events in the Life of Jesus Christ

*". . . good news of a great joy which
will come to all the people."*

Luke 2:10

When we come to consider how to introduce the child to the Bible we are immediately faced with the dilemma of whether to begin with the Old or the New Testament.[1] There is only one covenant between God and man, but it is realized in successive stages. Should we make the child retrace this development from its beginning? We have already replied in part to this question in chapter 3, where we stressed the centrality of the person of Christ in our catechesis. In our estimation, children should be initiated into their present religious reality, and fundamental to it is the presence of a Mediator through whom we go to the Father. Moreover, in order to approach the Old Testament it is necessary to be able to move easily within time, and to be able to imagine customs and habits different from our own. What impression would a child receive, for example, from the account of the sacrifice of Isaac, without knowing or being able to understand that there were cultures in which the offering of a son in sacrifice was an act deemed pleasing to their deity? We maintain that the children's initiation to the Old Testament should not begin before the age of eight. Further, we should not let ourselves be deceived by the *apparent facility* of many pages of the Bible.

In the Bible we find a vast abundance of facts, impressive and easy to recount. We should make an accurate choice of these to present to children, concentrating solely on the passages the theological meaning of which the child can penetrate. The Bible is a book of historical theology or theological history; we cannot separate theology from history in the Bible, for if we did we would be unfaithful to the message. There are many biblical passages the history of which the child easily learns, without piercing through to their theology. We should carefully avoid such passages, otherwise we risk making the Bible become a book of "stories" if not "tall tales." If, for example, we were to present a child with the account of original sin, it would be taken in the same way as a fairy tale where animals speak; however the child could in no sense understand its meaning or teaching. In our view it is a mistake to give children texts that are predominantly, if not exclusively, narrative in nature. As a matter of fact we think that the more articulated and detailed the narration, the greater the risk that it will obstruct the children from reaching its depth.

I do not think it right that the child first know certain facts, and only at a later time enter into their theological significance. I believe that an event learned only as a story (or legend) will stay a story even when the child is grown, and it will be extremely difficult to recover its theological content later on. The children's drawings can be a guide in our choice of texts: If the child, in relation to a specific biblical passage, only knows how to draw descriptive rather than interpretative illustrations, then it is better to avoid that text; it is obvious that his understanding of it has stayed on a level of superficiality. On the other hand, there are numerous biblical passages the child is capable of penetrating deeply; the richness of content in the drawings reproduced in this book proves this fact. Why not concentrate on texts such as these?

The Prophecies

With regard to the Old Testament, we have limited ourselves, up to the present, to giving children under six years of age a selection of a few, short, prophetic passages during the season of Advent. Prophetic language is composed of images and consequently it corresponds very well to the capacities of even young children. Isaiah has appeared to be especially striking:

The people who walked in darkness
have seen a great light;

those who dwelt in a land of deep darkness,
on them has light shined.

(Isaiah 9:1)

As we have seen, the child associates the images of Christ the Light and Christ the Good Shepherd and both, mutually completing one another, are impressed in the child's mind in an effaceable manner.

In the same year or in following years, depending on the children's age and receptive abilities, other short passages may be added; for example, the following verse from Isaiah that announces the one through whom the light will come to us: The light bearer will be a Child with wonderful names:

For to us a child is born,
to us a son is given;
and the government will be upon his shoulder,
and his name will be called
"Wonderful Counsellor, Mighty God,
Everlasting Father, Prince of Peace."

(Isaiah 9:6)

Catechists may find other passages that are just as striking. What seems important to us is that the texts be few in number, brief in length and formulated in images.

Other texts that we give gradually to the children are those that speak of the Mother of Christ:

Behold, a young woman shall conceive
and bear a son, and shall call his name Immanuel.

(Isaiah 7:14)

And also the passage that tells of the Messiah's birthplace:

But you, O Bethlehem,
who are little to be among
the clans of Judah,
from you shall come forth for me
one who is to be ruler in Israel.

(Micah 5:1)

In this text, Micah highlights the small-great contrast that plays such a large role in the Bible and is so impressive to the children (see chapter 8).

Our aim in giving these Old Testament texts is not to initiate the children into the Old Testament, which would require, as we said, a historical sensibility that children under the age of six cannot have. Our aim is to offer images and expressions that are striking to and readily grasped by the children. We will show later (chapter 7) how the various names of the Messiah (Isaiah 9:6) furnish the child with a language of prayer.

The New Testament: The Incarnation

With the exception of these few prophetic passages, we keep primarily to the New Testament, centering on the parables and the events of the birth, death, and resurrection of Christ. We greatly restrict our discussion of the miracles: It seems to us that the particular power Jesus manifested in working miracles should not be separated from the consideration of that power He continues to exercise through the Church. But to achieve this unity with the children has proved difficult up to the present. On the other hand, the miracles considered on their own can tempt the children, in our view, into the world of magic that many assert to be indivisible from the religiousness of the young child; however it is a quality we have never seen in children, except for that magic which has been induced by the adult (cf. chapters 7 and 11).

The events of Christ's infancy[2] appear rather difficult due to the misuse that is generally made of them by often telling them (with many diminutives!) as if they were beautiful fables. The fact is that the infancy narratives, especially in Luke, are a type of "theological embroidery"—if it is possible to call them so—whereby the evangelist stresses the grandeur of the mystery he is announcing through a variety of techniques.

These are pages of exceedingly rich theological content; their theology is neither systematic nor explicit but one that is almost "hidden" in the text. We are dealing with a theology that is completely different from the textbook kind of theology; it cannot be learned through academic study but rather gleaned through a prolonged "listening" to the text. It is a theology characteristically allusive. The evangelist alludes many times to a connection between the events he is speaking about and the history that has preceded them. It has been pointed out that the celestial messengers who address the Mother of God and the shepherds structure their speech basically along the lines of the prophetic proclamations: they invite us (1) not to be afraid, (2) because the Lord is near, and (3) to rejoice therefore.[3] See, for example, in Zephaniah:

> *Sing aloud,* O daughter of Sion;
> *shout,* O Israel!
> *Rejoice and exult* with all your heart,
> O daughter of Jerusalem!
>
> The Lord has taken away the judgments against you,
> he has cast out your enemies.
> The King of Israel, *the Lord is in your midst;*
> you shall fear evil no more.
>
> On that day it shall be said to Jerusalem:
> *Do not fear,* O Zion;
> let not your hands grow weak.
> The Lord your God is in your midst,
> a warrior who gives victory.
>
> (Zephaniah 3:14–17)

These elements are found in the Gospel of Luke as well: "*Rejoice,* full of grace, *the Lord is with you*"; "*Do not be afraid,* Mary" (Luke 1:28–30); and later in the words addressed to the shepherds: "*Be not afraid;* for behold I bring you good news of a *great joy* which will come to all the people; for to you is born this day in the city of David a Savior, who is *Christ the Lord*" (Luke 2:10–11). The references are apparent, and it is through allusions such as these that the evangelist tells us, or, better, lets us discover, that the new event he is proclaiming is the conclusive link in a long chain of events to which it is in some way connected. The allusion is clear but not explicit, so the text leaves room for our own search and joy of discovery. In this way, we become accustomed to discovering, in the literary form of biblical passages, the "signs" of the mystery. It is not possible to speak to the young child—with whom it is inadvisable to increase the number of Old Testament passages—of the connection we mentioned.

Nevertheless, knowing this relation will help catechists to redis-
cover the greatness of the infancy narratives, which perhaps is
not always obvious to us.

The Lucan texts we have been speaking about also emphasize a great contrast; many expressions have an awesome grandeur, others refer to a very simple reality: The Child is spoken of
as the "Son of the Most High," "Son of God," and "The Lord God
will give to him the throne of his father David, and he will reign
over the house of Jacob forever, and of his kingdom there will be
no end"; He is the "Savior" and the evangelist calls him by the
name of "Lord," that name which the Old Testament reserved
jealously for God alone; stars and celestial powers move around
the crib. But at the same time it is said of Him: "You will find a
babe wrapped in swaddling cloths"; the Evangelist Matthew
says: Mary "had borne a son" and "called his name Jesus" (Matthew 1:25). These contrasts are not without significance; they
bring us face to face with the wonderful reality of the Child: son
of woman, like each one of us, and Son of God!

The catechist should have this contrast in mind when speaking with the children, so as to lead them to ask themselves, full of
wonder: But who can this Child be? In this way we will accustom
the children to the fact that the biblical text contains something
to be discovered, which is to be read in depth, which is not readily exhaustible. In this way we will educate the children to humility in facing the Word of God.

Meditation and Prayer on the Mystery of the Incarnation

We begin our presentation of the infancy narratives in the
same way as the parables: presenting the episodes one at a time,
narrating the events in our own words, and reading the Gospel
text solemnly. We should also accustom ourselves to a "living"
reading of the text; that is, we should feel ourselves personally
involved in the listening and the response to the text.[4] The reflection that follows the reading is for this purpose; for instance:
"The words the angel proclaimed to the Mother of God are addressed to us as well, to me too. How shall we respond? Mary expressed her joy saying: 'My soul magnifies the Lord!' Her joy is
mine too; it is 'a great joy which will come to all the people.' And
how shall I express it? The shepherds were the first to know that
a Savior was born, 'who is Christ the Lord.' They searched for
Him and found a 'babe lying in a manger' with His mother be-

side Him. The shepherds were astonished and happy, and they glorified and praised God. The Magi came to the crib after a long journey. They knelt down before Him, they worshipped Him and brought Him gifts. But now we too are around the crib. I am here too. What shall we do? What shall we say?"

In order to facilitate and support personal expression, we introduce some examples of prayer. Each of the infancy narratives contains a prayer: in the angel's words to the Mother of God we have the beginning of the Hail Mary; the Magnificat is the song of thanksgiving on the occasion of the visit to Elizabeth; the angels sing the Gloria at Christ's birth; during the presentation in the Temple the aged Simeon prays the Nunc Dimittis, the second part of which is a magnificent hymn to Christ the Light, which may be given to the children:

> A light to enlighten the pagans
> and the glory of your people Israel.
>
> (Luke 2:32)

Such examples should be offered to the children with great discretion so as not to stifle their own personal prayer. If we wish to give the Magnificat, for instance, we restrict ourselves to suggesting only the first verse:

> My soul magnifies the Lord,
> and my spirit rejoices in God my Savior.
>
> (Luke 1:46–47)

We give a text like this as one example among many of the ways one may respond to God, as a stimulus to personal prayer, so that each person finds in his own heart his response to the Lord Who speaks to His creatures (cf. chapter 7).

In the presentation of the parables, the reflection following the narration of the text usually leads to meditation and through it to prayer. The reflection that follows the narration of the historical events has shown itself to be a more direct initiation to personal prayer. The presentation of the events surrounding Christ's birth easily gives rise to celebrations in the true and real sense of the word: In the Advent season, for instance, following the presentation of the prophetic proclamations, we may encourage a "procession of waiting" in which the children carry the statue of the Mother of God; during Christmas time, there may be a procession with the Child and Mother, linked to the reading of the Gospel text; after Christmas, as a kind of Epiphany celebration, there is the offering of the gifts of gold, frankincense, and myrrh and other gifts in general, and so on. At other times the younger children, with the older children's help, will dramatize events relating to the infancy narratives.

For the child's personal work on the infancy narratives, there is a material composed of a series of miniature reconstructed scenes, one for each event, almost like an advanced manger scene or diorama, which the children work with in small groups or individually. This material is prepared according to a criterion different from that used for the parable material: The figures are three-dimensional, and the historical character of these events permits and requires research into details, not indicated by the text, that make the scene more living. The difference between parable and historical events should be clear even from the material itself. The material reconstructions of the infancy-narrative series help the children who do not know how to read to recall the biblical content. The older children have at their disposal, as well as the material, a set of Gospel booklets, one for each event; the children read the text and construct the scene at the same time. The events we present to the children are the Annunciation, the Visitation, the Adoration of the Shepherds, the Adoration of the Magi, the Presentation in the Temple, and the Flight into Egypt.

The depth of the children's penetration of the mystery of the Incarnation is shown in their prayer, such as Carlo (six years old) who prayed before the Child's crib: "I say to him: Alleluia to the mighty God." Expressions like these are a warning for us not to use baby talk with children, not to minimize what they know how to receive in all its greatness. We have observed how easily we speak in diminutives, whereas the child speaks of "the mighty God."

In their drawings, the children do not limit themselves to drawing the crib; rather they give it a theological interpretation. In drawing number 36, the figure depicted over the stable is intended to be the Holy Spirit. The young artist of drawing number 37 has achieved a most interesting synthesis: The birth is linked to Easter, indicated by the lighted paschal candle, and to our participation in the mystery, represented by the baptismal symbols of the cross and white gown. Both of these drawings were done by children around eleven years of age who live in the steppes of

Chad. The same connection between Christmas and Easter is found in drawings 38, 39, and 40, illustrated by five-year-old children during the Christmas season in different centers in Rome. In these drawings note the prevalence of the color yellow, which expresses joy, and the representation of Jesus on the cross, but He is alive. In the drawing of four-year-old Giulio, the nativity star dominates his illustration of the Last Supper (fig. 47). Maria Azzurra (five years old) has drawn a lighted candle on either side of the child Jesus, reminiscent of an altar, which indicates an obvious link between the birth of Jesus and the Messiah (fig. 44).

The drawings in which the children unite the child Jesus and the Good Shepherd (figs. 41, 42) are another demonstration that the children do not stop at the fact itself, but rather through it they contemplate the mystery of Christ's person. Even more remarkable is the connection between the nativity and the Mass that can be seen in drawing no. 46, where the child Jesus "dreams" of the altar. In a Christmas drawing, Abi (five and a half years old) has illustrated the child Jesus shining with light—an element that likens him to the risen Christ, the Good Shepherd, and the bread and wine, also radiating light (fig. 45).

Biblical Geography

In our view it is important that the historical events also have materials relative to their geographical reconstruction in order to let the children know how to situate them in a point in space. This material helps to concretize the events. Therefore we present a globe of the world on which all the dry land is colored white and only one miniscule red point is marked out: the land of Israel. For the events surrounding the birth, we use a plastic relief model of Palestine to scale: First we indicate the three principal cities of Nazareth, Bethlehem, and Jerusalem; then we gradually localize and name the regions and other cities named in the Gospel; finally we highlight the topographical features. We follow a process that is the reverse of what is generally used in the study of geography, because the interest this country holds for us is primarily historical; thus the geography depends on the history.

In relation to the Easter-Pentecost events, we concentrate our study on the city of Jerusalem. We have built a relief model of the city to scale for the children to use. The historical buildings and city walls are movable; they can be isolated and reas-

sembled on a large cardboard that outlines the exact dimensions
of the plastic model. This is the way the children learn the names
of the places where the most important events of the passion,
death, and resurrection took place.

With regard to the events of the passion, we restrict ourselves to indicating the location of the Cenacle, the house of Cai-
aphas, the Antonia Tower, the Temple, the Garden of Olives,
Calvary, and the tomb of the resurrection. The texts offer a detailed account of the passion; but we believe these texts should
not be given to children. At times these passages go into details
that arouse horror, such as we could not bear in relation to anyone dear to us; why then should we dwell on them with respect to
Jesus? We risk inciting sentiments that should not be aroused.
We concentrate on the Last Supper,[5] the death and resurrection,[6] and the gift of the Holy Spirit.

The presentation of the Last Supper is integrated with what
has been presented previously on the Mass, especially in relation
to the epiclesis. During the Last Supper presentation we emphasize Jesus' will to remain with men of all times; therefore we focus on the words of the consecration with which He expressed
this will, designating as the ultimate end of the bread and wine
that they be the signs of His perpetual presence in the midst of
mankind and of His continuing intervention in the life of hu-
manity.

The material for the children's personal work on the Last
Supper presentation consists of a wooden reconstruction of the
environment: a small model of the Cenacle, a table, small three-
dimensional figures of Jesus and the apostles, the bread and
wine, and the Gospel text. We read principally Mark 14:12–17,
22–24, omitting the betrayal of Judas, which leaves too strong an
impression on the younger children. The children work with the
material in the usual way, reading the Gospel booklet and moving the figures.

The Last Supper is another event that readily lends itself to
be celebrated by the younger children themselves, along with the
older ones. A small group of twelve children gathers around a table; each child chooses the name of an apostle. One child is en-
trusted with the task of saying the words of Jesus, which are
written, depending on the age of the children, more or less according to the structure of the Jewish paschal banquet. When
the supper is concluded, another child reads an abbreviated account of the death and resurrection. The actualization follows

immediately afterward: Crucifix and lighted candles are brought to the table, transforming it into an altar; the circle of children widens to include all who are present. The children often linger for long periods of time around the improvised altar and express their prayer spontaneously.

The Death and Resurrection

The time when we come to speak of Christ's death and resurrection is the moment when the Good Shepherd parable is rooted in history. We have already said how the children intuitively grasp the paschal import of the parable. The Good Shepherd is always at the disposition of mankind, and this constant attitude of His is concretized in a particular way at the moment of His death.

For a number of reasons we hold especially to the Lucan version of Christ's death (23:33–49). It is in Luke above all that we find the great pursuit of contrasts: he records the supreme moment of the humiliation of Jesus with frequent references to His kingship (verses 37–38, 42). Jesus is king of a mysterious kingdom, one that is even like a mustard seed, so much so that at times it is difficult for us to see it; He is king on the cross as well. Luke explicitly cites Jesus' words of forgiveness, and also His power to convert in regard to the good thief and the centurion— an element to which the children are most sensitive. Naturally our choice of Luke is not exclusive. John's account (19:17–30) offers us the opportunity of pointing out the presence of the pagans (the soldiers) and Jews (the Mother of God, John) around the cross of Christ, and therefore to emphasize once again the universality of the event and—with the older children only—the shared responsibility of each of us for Christ's death.

Nonetheless the proclamation of the death of Christ should never be disjoined from the announcement of His resurrection. We believe it is necessary to tie them together; we do not even pause temporarily on the death alone, considering perhaps it a well-known fact that the death was followed by the resurrection. Yes, it is known, but the fact is that very often the accent is applied to the death and so it comes to assume a greater vividness than the resurrection. The disturbing proclamation we give is of the resurrection, and it is on this that we should concentrate. Death is a common event; many men have had the courage to face death for love of their brothers. What is absolutely new is that, in Jesus, death is followed by renewed and eternal life. What we find so hard to grasp is the fact that, in Christ, life is stronger than death. To us it seems appropriate to avoid long accounts of the passion, in order to balance the length of the passion narration with the account of the resurrection.

As for the resurrection texts, it appeared suitable to us to follow our preference for Luke once again, especially in relation to the striking passage: "Why do you seek the living among the dead? He is not here, but has risen" (Luke 24:5). We also read John's account because of its vivacity and the importance granted to Peter.

The presentation of the paschal events follows the same sequence as the infancy narratives: the narration of the details of the event, the solemn reading of the Gospel text, followed by the children's personal participation, as in the parable and infancy narrative presentations. There is however a difference: As we have seen, the parables lead especially to meditation and through it to prayer; the infancy narratives lead more directly to personal and spontaneous prayer; the paschal events adapt themselves especially to be lived by the children in more structured celebrations. Given the great wealth of the paschal Liturgy, these celebrations frequently retrace the great services of Holy Week and the Easter triduum; as such, they become a direct initiation into the Liturgy of the Church.

The Liturgy of Light

The children live the proclamation of the death and resurrection especially in the Liturgy of Light (cf. chapter 7), which, through the contrast between darkness and light, involves us dramatically in the fundamental event in the Good Shepherd's life. Based on the observation of numerous children's drawings, we can say that the Liturgy of Light prevails over the historical approach; that is to say, once again the children interpret the events theologically rather than chronicling them.

In the drawing of Valerio (five years old), the crucifix is placed to one side of the page, the remainder of which is completely filled with blazing lights (fig. 43). In Roberto's drawing, there is the figure of the crucified Christ, and also the risen Lord represented in two ways: in the paschal candle and as Christ the Light; the light is also shared by a little boy and girl, with the written explanation: "The boy holds the candle in his hand. He has life like the risen Jesus" (fig. 31). Note that the crucifixion has been illustrated on the lower part of the page with the paschal candle placed directly beside it; the figure of the risen Jesus, haloed with light, dominates the upper portion of the sheet. In many other drawings the children entirely omit the depiction of the historical event, illustrating only the paschal candle.

Pentecost

When we come to Pentecost, near the end of our catechetical year, the children already have a profound familiarity with the Holy Spirit. Our catechesis is Christocentric, as we have said, but it is obviously Christological-Trinitarian. The person of the Father is illumined particularly through the Mass: It is the Father who sends us the gift of Christ's presence, and it is to the Father that we make our offering as the expression of our gratitude. We also speak of the Father especially in relation to the Annunciation (the Father sends the messenger), and during the presentation of Baptism in the sign of the cross, the sacramental words, and so forth.

With regard to the Holy Spirit, it is striking to see the facility with which the children enter into relationship with Him. The Holy Spirit's work appears obvious to them, and they know how to recognize it spontaneously in the most important moments. The children come to know the Holy Spirit through the historical life of Jesus—it is through the Spirit that Jesus was born and raised from the dead—and also through the liturgies of the Eucharist and Baptism. Therefore, the children know the Holy Spirit's work both in the person of Jesus Christ Himself and in His continuing work within the Church. Franca (six years old) wrote on the back of her drawing of the risen Christ: "The Holy Spirit made Jesus be born. When He rose the Holy Spirit gave Him more light. Good girls have gone to heaven and the Holy Spirit has given light to Jesus' sheep too." What has been particularly enlightening for the children in relation to the Holy Spirit is to see His action in the Eucharistic presence. When we hit on this point there was what Montessori would have called an "explosion": Starting with this essential aspect, the children then knew how to see with ease the Spirit's many other manifestations.

Catechesis on Pentecost does not present difficulties, therefore. We proceed as usual, narrating the event and reading the text from the second chapter of the Acts of the Apostles. The children also live this event, for the most part, through celebration (see chapter 7). The material consists of the scripture booklet, the reconstruction of the Cenacle used in the Last Supper presentation, and the figures of the apostles and the Mother of God.

In concluding we would like to say that the presentation of sacred scripture—parables or historical narratives—should never be disunited from prayer, in a structured or unstructured form. The proclamation is complete when it has been received, and, in one form or another, when it has been given a response.

At this point we quote the following from a catechist's diary (Rome, Via Casilina, First Class) as an example of the position the Holy Spirit occupies in the children's discussions:

Q: Who gave life back to the Good Shepherd?
A: The Holy Spirit (a little girl responded immediately with complete certainty). It was a new life . . . of light . . . that gives joy.
Q: Then where did Jesus go?
A: To heaven. Of course, with that beautiful life!
Q: But did He want to stay there alone?
A: With the Father . . . with the Holy Spirit . . . with the sheep too . . . and with the Madonna . . . the sheep should follow the Shepherd.
Q: How can the sheep get to heaven?
A: The Holy Spirit helps us too (the actual words of the little girl). The Holy Spirit comes to bring us Jesus' life.
Q: When did He give it to us?
A: When we received baptism . . . but He gives it to me when I am with Jesus . . . when I am praying in church.
Q: The Holy Spirit is in church . . . in the tabernacle . . . . We already know that in the tabernacle there is . . . ?
A: Jesus! Jesus and the Holy Spirit are never apart. Jesus and the Holy Spirit are in our hearts . . . you don't see them.
Q: Who finds them?
A: The person who pays attention.
Q: How does one pay attention?
A: With the heart . . . with our life too . . . thinking and listening to the Holy Spirit's words.
A: If a little girl stays at her place really quiet she hears Him.

Then the lesson on Pentecost followed. At the end of it, because we were late, the children proposed to reorder everything in absolute silence, to go out silently so they could listen to the Holy Spirit, and if someone's mother had not yet come they would wait alone to one side.

NOTES

1. C. Bissoli, *La Bibbia nella Catechesi* (Torino-Leumann: LDC, 1972).

2. A. Feuillet, *Jésus et sa Mère* (Paris: Gabalda, 1973).

3. S. Lyonnet, "Il racconto dell'annunciazione e la maternità divina della Madonna," *La Scuola Cattolica* (1954), pp. 1–38.

4. R. Marle, *Herméneutique et Catéchèse* (Paris: Fayard-Mame, 1970); by the same author, "La préoccupation herméneutique en catéchèse," *Lumen Vitae* (1970), pp. 377–382. F. Bovon, *Problèmes de méthode en sciences bibliques,* Université de Génève, s.n., pp. 24ff.

5. J. Jeremias, *The Eucharistic Words of Jesus* (London: S.C. M. Press, 1966). Italian Edition, *Le parole dell'Ultima Cena* (Brescia: Paideia, 1967). German Edition, *Die Abendmahlsworte Jesu* (Göttingen: Vandenhoeck & Ruprecht, 1949).

6. A. Ammassari, *La risurrezione nell'insegnamento, nella profezia, nelle apparizioni di Gesù* (Roma: Città Nuova Editrice, Vol. 1, 1975, Vol. 2, 1976).

Chapter Seven
Prayer

"By the mouths of children, babes in arms,
You set a stronghold firm against your foes."

Psalm 8:2

Prayer has a special importance in the life of children, both because of the great capacity they have shown in this realm and because, not yet participating fully at Mass, prayer is the principal way they nourish their baptismal life and prepare, at the same time, for active involvement in the Mass, the highest and most complete form of prayer. Education to prayer is fundamental to the catechesis of young children.

If we want to help children's prayer we should first of all become aware of *how* they pray. The diversity between the religious life of adult and child, which we have already mentioned (chapter 2) forbids us to impose our own prayer guidelines on children. We risk leading them along a path that is not theirs. We risk extinguishing the spontaneous expression of their relationship with God and give rise to the idea that when we pray we say certain fixed things, without necessarily adhering to them within ourselves. We could separate prayer from life in children.

Once again the adult sees the need to step aside in order to allow the children to really express themselves and, if possible, to glean the secret of their prayer. This is what we have been able to see: Children pray with great facility; we find they are always disposed to prayer, which can be a time of special enchantment for them. Maria Montessori recounted that she was holding a little girl of eighteen months in her arms when the midday church bells began to ring; she prayed slowly: "Hail Mary, full of grace"; the little girl responded: "How beautiful. Say it again."

120

The prayer was repeated with solemnity several more times, always in the same few words. At the end the little girl said: "How beautiful. When I go home I'll tell it to Mommy." We have already spoken of Stefania, who finished her prayer with the words: "My body is happy." For children, prayer does not mean only verbal expression; they live the words of the psalm: "Praise is silence for thee, O God" (Psalm 65:1). Sometimes in praying with children one experiences moments of such rich, full silence! In cases like these we do not think that it would be an exaggeration to speak of true contemplation.

How Children Pray

For the most part, children's prayer is expressed with few words, in short and essential phrases. We include here two examples of prayer, from two different groups of children, from two different catechetical centers. In both instances the prayers were recorded by someone seated close to the children.

The prayer following the first presentation of Baptism, Catechetical Center, Via degli Orsini:

Thank you for the light (Stefania).
Thank you, Jesus, for giving us our hearts.
Thank you, Jesus, for giving us our joy.
Thank you for giving us our life.
Thank you for creating the whole world.
Thank you, Jesus, for giving life to me and everyone else.
Thank you, Jesus, for creating everyone and for giving us life.
Thank you, Jesus, for making our houses too, and when it rains we take cover in our houses.
Thank you, Jesus, for baptizing us.
Thank you for giving us all our life.
Thank you, Jesus, for making us be born in the sheepfold.
Thank you for giving us that beautiful gift.
Thank you for giving us the gift.
Thank you for creating everyone.
Thank you, Jesus, for creating us in the sheepfold.
Thank you, Jesus, for when we die we go to paradise.
Thank you, Jesus, for always giving us light.

Thank you, Jesus, for sending us this light from heaven
right into our hearts.
Thank you for giving us bread.
Thank you for giving us everything.
Thank you for giving us wine and holy water.
Thank you, Jesus, for giving us food to eat.
Thank you for making plants and wheat.
Thank you for making soup too.
Thank you for creating us all.
Thank you, Jesus, for making us strong and good.
Thank you for making us work.
Thank you for leading us into our beautiful sheepfold.
Thank you because we are your sheep.
Thank you for coming into our hearts.
My body is happy (Stefania).

The prayer following the same presentation, Our Lady of
Lourdes Center (Tormarancia, Rome):

Jesus, you gave us light.
Jesus, I am all yours.
Thank you for the gift.
Thank you for the beautiful gift.
Thank you for everything.
Thank you for creating us.
Thank you for the gift.
Jesus, thank you, because I am one of your sheep.
Jesus, thank you, for leading us into the sheepfold.
Jesus, I want to be good.
Jesus, thank you, for always coming to look for us.
Thank you, Jesus, for making me one of your sheep.
My grandmother is dead, but I'm happy she is with Je-
sus.

Examples of this kind are numerous. Rather than the loqua-
cious and structured prayer we might perhaps expect, the child
offers us instead gleams of prayer. At times like these, every
child expresses his own personal prayer; the expression of one
child or another is quite often interspaced with long intervals of
silence, during which the adult is frequently led to believe that
the prayer is finished. The adult should learn how to wait, convinced that silence is also prayer, and that it is in silence that the

spoken expression germinates. The adult should learn to be respectful of the child's rhythm, which is much slower than our own.

From these examples it is evident how mistaken it is for the adult to give long prayer formulae to children; they are contrary to their mode of expression. The prayer of children up to the age of seven or eight is almost exclusively prayer of thanksgiving and praise. The adult who tries to lead the child to prayers of petition falsifies and distorts the child's religious expression. The child feels no need to ask because he knows himself to be in the peaceful possession of certain goods.

Here are some other examples, recorded as they were spoken by a group of children between four and six years of age:

—Jesus is handsome, he is handsome!
—Jesus, you put a light in our hearts that is more beautiful and bigger than the sun.
—You are a king who rules over love.
—Jesus, you are a tree that lasts forever, all the todays and all the tomorrows.

Another child prays in rhyme:

Gesù, sei grande, sei buono, sei bello:
tu per me sei un gioiello.
(Jesus, you are great, you are good, you are handsome:
to me you are a jewel.)

Emanuela (five years old) led a group of thirty children in prayer. Their ages ranged from one to six years (Adele Costa Gnocchi Children's house, photo 6). The silence was most impressive as she prayed in a sing-song voice:

Jesus has given children
He created everything.
He gave life to fathers and mothers.
Everyone has life,
Jesus is risen
and everyone has life.
Jesus is risen
and everyone is good.
Because God said so

because God said so to everyone,
and then He said: Let there be children
and let there be fathers and mothers too
and let there be fathers too.
Because Jesus is good, He is good,
because to everyone—He gave life
everyone—He gave life.
And God said: light,
and the light was lit,
and He said: This is my light.
And God created
the creatures of God
and all the children who have a first name and a
last name and the children,
and He created Jesus.
Goodbye, Jesus.

Another older child (four years old) prays:

Thank you, Jesus, for putting our white gowns on us
when we were little.

A prayer of praise that is synthetically very powerful was recorded from the lips of a three-year-old boy:

Goodness, light. Amen.

Some country children of Colonna (Rome) were praying together
and their thanksgiving encompassed all the goods of the world,
from the most transcendent to the most everyday:

Jesus, you are my shepherd.
You are my savior.
Jesus, you are my father.
You are my friend.
Jesus, you are the king of the world.
Jesus, you help me, thank you.
Jesus, I thank you for giving us all these things.
Jesus, I thank you for making us live and letting us play
with our friends.
Thank you, Jesus, for creating us.
Thank you, Jesus, for giving us our mother and father.

Thank you for giving us all these churches and making us civilized and Christians.
Thank you for giving us all our strengths.
Thank you, Jesus, for giving us such a beautiful sky and such beautiful stars.
Thank you for giving us legs for walking and playing football.
Thank you, Jesus, for giving us little cousins and a brother.

The prayer continued with thanksgiving for the Lord who gave us mouths to eat and hands to touch, an aunt, playing fields and having fun, grandmother and grandfather, school for studying and learning many things, the teacher, medicine for healing, houses to live in, and concluded with these words:

Thank you, God, for letting us live in this world
and for letting us live like civilized people.

After listening to the Pentecost narration, a group of five- and six-year old children dictated the following prayer to the catechist to be read afterward in church:

Come, Holy Spirit,
give us the strength to be happy.
We thank you for giving us baptism.
Come, Lord,
we await you with big hearts,
and give us the strength to hold ourselves in hope.
Be calm,
for the Holy Spirit will come.
Thank you, Holy Spirit,
I won't ever chase you from my heart again.
Come, Holy Spirit,
and put your love in our hearts
and in everyone.

Here is the prayer dictated by another group for the same purpose; this time, however, the children are between the ages of four and five:

Dear Jesus, you are our king and you are so good.
You are our Shepherd.

You are the Son of God.
You are the Son of Mary, who is our mother too;
she is so good and beautiful, she blessed us and she
taught us to pray.
You are our Savior.
Thanks to you, Creator, for giving us everything,
for giving us the sea, the little birds, and all the beautiful things.
Thank you for giving us food to eat.
I love you so much, because you are the Shepherd and
we are your sheep. Amen.

In praying, children express the sense of God's transcendence and His nearness at the same time. Superlatives occur often in their prayer: "You are light greater than the world's";
"You give me joy which doesn't exist anywhere in the whole
world"; "Jesus, not even the snow is whiter than your soul"; but
the child also says: "Jesus does things with us."

Two children, both five years of age, were praying together;
one prayed: "Thank you for coming into our hearts, because now
we can pray to you inside us"; the other child continued: "Yes,
He's really great company and we will never be alone." The joy
of the relationship with God is expressed in offering as well:

Everything that is most beautiful in the world, I prefer
to give to you.
I give you my whole world, which is my heart.
Jesus, at night before going to bed, I give you a gown all
golden, full of perfumed flowers, but it's only for you, all
for you.

A little girl turned to the figure of the child Jesus and said:

I want to make you a little house all of gold.

A rare example of a prayer of petition (five-year-old child):

Jesus, come; spread your light in all the world.

The experience of three-and-a-half year old Claudia is a remarkable example of the child's capacity to prolong prayer

(Adele Costa Gnocchi Children's House, Rome). The little girl accompanied a visitor to the atrium and described all its furnishings to her; then the child sat down and took a small Gospel booklet, pretending to read it. The visitor, standing close to the miniature altar, joined her hands together. "Why are you holding your hands like that?" asked Claudia. "Because I am praying," replied the visitor, to which Claudia responded: "Then kneel down." The guest obeyed, and the little girl turned to her and began suggesting the words: "Lord, Lord"; then Claudia started to pray: "The Lord is my shepherd, I shall not want," interspersed between moments of silence. This continued for about ten minutes, at which point the visitor, thinking her presence to be an influence on the child, withdrew to the adjoining room from which she could hear and at times see the child without being seen herself.

Claudia resumed her prayer without indicating any awareness of the visitor's absence. The child continued to repeat and to sing softly to herself: "The Lord is my shepherd, I shall not want," interspersed with long intervals of complete silence. Only once did she change the words: Taking an image enclosed in a frame, she opened it and said: "Hello, Jesus, how are you?" but then she returned again to the words of the psalm. At a certain moment a little boy opened the atrium door and then banged it with a crash. Claudia got up, went to the door, opened it, and said: "Close it slowly," and then she went back to praying a prayer composed equally of words and silence.

It will hardly be believed, but Claudia continued to pray for an hour and a half. The joy she manifested after she left the atrium was proof that she had had a deeply gratifying experience; she went over to embrace the directress—something totally unlike Claudia—and said to her: "I prayed so much!"

Magical Prayer

If children's prayer is—as it is—essentially thanksgiving and praise, it cannot be magical in nature. I realize I am making an affirmation in contrast to what has been stated by eminent scholars in this field; however, the fact is that in more than twenty-five years of observation I have not seen magical prayer in children, that is, a prayer that tends to bend the divine will to one's own advantage. It may be interesting to note what G. Milanesi posits at the conclusion of his long work of research on this subject:

> It is not daring to think that for many children the rate of interest in magic is noticeably lowered by a more liberating educational direction. The conclusion would be, at this point, that magical thought is proper to those persons who are, to a greater or lesser degree, maladjusted, unsatisfied, incomplete. It is more a symptom of immaturity than an indicator of normality.[1]

Therefore, magic in the child would not necessarily be the manifestation of his incapacity to attain higher levels, as some scholars would have us suppose. Instead, magic would appear to be a deviated manifestation, an indicator of an encounter with God that is not satisfying, or, better, an indication that the person of God has not been presented in a way that satisfies the child. Hence, we ask ourselves if that magic, which so many people have seen in children, could not derive from a manner of giving the kerygma that is not sufficiently "liberating," according to Milanesi's term, and also from the habit of many adults who lead children to prayer of petition.

How to Help Children's Prayer

If this is the situation of the child's prayer, what then can the adult do? It is clear that we intend to speak about education to *prayer* and not to *prayers*. In teaching prayers, often we do not initiate children into prayer, that certain interior agility by which the heart turns to God to listen and respond to Him. Prayer is the most personal and jealous expression of the relationship with God; no one can really teach another to pray. Much less here than for the other points set forth in this book do we intend to give exact indications that are to be followed to the letter. In this sphere, even more than in the other areas we have been speaking about, the catechist should call forth all his respect for the mystery and for the child, and for all the child's sensitivity and creativity.

In our consideration, what the adult can do is to establish the premises that will help prayer to arise. Such premises should be as indirect in character as possible, so as to allow the greatest space for the child's personal response.

The "Kerygma"

Prayer, before it is the response of the person, is first the listening to God; thus we believe the "kerygma" is the departure point for an initiation to prayer. We could say that everything we say and do with the children during our catechetical meetings is preparation for prayer, insofar as it tends to facilitate the encounter with God, to help us become conscious of the gifts we have received, and therefore to elicit a response. We can say that every time an important point is proclaimed during our meetings with the children, the listening spontaneously becomes prayer. The richer the kerygma, the more living its proclamation, the more the children will welcome it with joy and wonder and the richer will their response be. Without the proclamation, or faced with a proclamation that is impoverished and "minimized," prayer will be empty and lifeless.

The kerygma is therefore the means with which the catechist is enabled to give the child's prayer the necessary nourishment: knowledge of God's word and His great deeds with regard to man, leaving the child to find his own response. It is the task of the adult who is constantly close to the child to exercise that inner agility we mentioned in reference to the events of everyday life, transforming some joy, good news, or happy occasion into prayer. The tasks of catechist and parent are distinct and complementary: Without the help of parents, prayer risks becoming removed from the child's personal everyday life, by concentrating too exclusively on certain areas even if they are the great gestures of God in the history of mankind; without the catechist, there is the danger that prayer will become impoverished within confines that are too limited and too personalized.

Prayer Formulae

When we approach the realm of prayer expression, the problem of formulae arises. Is it good to give prayer formulae to children, or is it better to omit them completely with young children for fear they will suffocate their own personal impulse to pray?

We think formulae may be a useful means in the education to prayer; nevertheless, it is not without dangers. In our estimation, formulae should not be given until we are sure the child has that interior agility we mentioned, through which prayer is a genuine and spontaneous expression. An untimely use of formu-

lae can stifle the child's personal expression and send his spirit
into the worst of sleeps. When a child is encouraged to pray, after
the presentation of the Good Shepherd parable for instance, and
he responds: "I will say the Hail Mary to Him," there is no prayer
in him. When a child like this understands that he must pray,
there is a type of spring within him that is set off automatically,
so that he repeats phrases worn out with use, which do not relate
in any way to his interior state. In this case, to give the child
more formulae would mean burdening him with a baggage of
words that have lost any resonance whatsoever in his heart; it
would mean putting the child's spirit into an even deeper sleep.

We have already replied in part to the question of how to
give prayer formulae—if the child's condition so advises—when
we remarked that the child prays with very short sentences.
Lengthy formulae are therefore in contrast to the child's way of
praying; the child will be lost in long formulae and will end up
repeating them without any inner adherence to their meaning.
The eighteen-month-old girl Maria Montessori wrote about was
captivated in listening to *one* phrase of the Hail Mary, simply because it was so short. This is why we begin by giving only a few
words to the child which can grow along with him.

To the young child who is meeting the Good Shepherd for
the first time, we offer only a single verse of Psalm 23: "The Lord
is my shepherd, I shall not want." Then we add the following
verses, a few at a time over an extended period; the second portion of the psalm, which repeats the content of the first part but
in convivial form, is saved until a later time:

> You prepare a table before me
> under the eyes of my enemies;
> you anoint my head with oil,
> my cup brims over.
>
> (Psalm 23:5)

This verse is especially suited to the period of first communion
preparation, and it may always be linked to the presentation of
the Mass. We give these very short passages so that the child can
listen to them, begin to make them his own, and transcribe them
if he wishes to and knows how to write. We do not spoil it by
making children memorize; this will happen naturally through

the spontaneous repetition of a passage that is particularly striking.

It is our custom to present prayer formulae in connection with a point of kerygma as one form among the many possible responses to what God has given us to know. Then the children are encouraged to add their own personal response (cf. chapter 6). During the celebration of the Liturgy of Light, for example, we offer the initial verse of Psalm 27:

> The Lord is my light and my salvation;
> whom shall I fear?
> The Lord is the stronghold of my life;
> of whom shall I be afraid?

Then we reflect with the child: "These words were once prayed by a devout Jew. Today, what shall we say?" Only with the older children do we give the remaining verses, which contain the image of war, where the devoted Israelite professes his faith in the Lord.

We also use a similar system with the formulae of great prayers, such as the Our Father. We propose the following words to the youngest children, who are just coming to know the first parables of the kingdom:

> Our Father who art in heaven
> Thy kingdom come.

With the older children who are in the stage of moral interests we highlight the words:

> Forgive us our debts
> As we also have forgiven our debtors.

Prayer suggested in this way may be said or sung.

When the formulae are offered in this manner they enrich the expression of prayer and provide a wealth of imagery and language that aid the child's own personal expression. Even if the children love to hear the same words over and over, there should also be a wide selection of formulae for their use; the opportunity to choose helps the child's inner adhesion to what is being said.

The Language of Prayer

In relation to prayer expression, we think something may be done also on the level of language; by this we mean providing the child with single words with which he may build his own prayer. We hope that research such as this, which has just been begun, may be continued and deepened.

It is obvious that prayer, which should be an expression of the Christian's whole life, is expressed in words from everyday life. Nevertheless, every human activity, interior and exterior, has in some way its own vocabulary, which does not enclose the individual action in a separate compartment but helps to express its unity. Of course formulae may be an aid to the expression of prayer, as we said; however, in formulae the thought is already formed, the "painting" is in some sense already drawn. Before presenting them with the finished painting, we believe that children can be furnished with the "single colors." As a matter of fact the children have shown themselves to be especially sensitive from the point of view of language when presented with specific texts; for instance, the prophetic names assigned to the Messiah in Isaiah (9:6) return frequently in their prayer:

Wonderful Counsellor, Mighty God,
Everlasting Father, Prince of Peace.

Other names of interest to the children are found in texts relating to the Mother of God: "Son of the Most High," "Son of God"; and from the Magnificat: "the Almighty," "Holy One."

The child appropriates these terms and adapts them in the structuring of his own personal prayer. We think that a similar work of "nomenclature" may be done with children under three years of age, that is, during the period when the child builds his own vocabulary and is avid to learn new words.

The Environment

We can help children's prayer through external conditions as well. The room for catechesis should not be without a prayer space. In this area there should be images, preferably three-dimensional for the youngest children, which can be changed in relation to the presentation of the various themes, and thus in accordance with the liturgical year. The passage from one liturgical season to another can be highlighted by changing the prayer cloth to the corresponding liturgical color; these changes should be done by the children themselves, in a solemn way. Special furnishings, such as a small cushion or prayer rug, as is the Eastern custom, may also invite the children to stay on their own in the prayer area. The children should have the opportunity of caring for this space, arranging flowers in vases, lighting the candles, and so forth. It is recommended that the lighting in this area of the atrium be adjustable so that it can be darkened to allow an atmosphere where the children may recollect themselves in candlelight alone. The prayer area is not a substitute for chapel or church, but it is a very important place for the education to prayer because it is here—more than in a chapel or church—that the child is completely comfortable, and his expression will be easier and more spontaneous. Actually, the most beautiful and genuine prayers are given birth to in the prayer area more than anywhere else, whereas it can happen that the style of apparatus usually associated with church or chapel may block the child's prayer, or at least render it more labored and difficult.

Fixed Hours of Prayer

As to the hours of prayers, we think that a constant religious recall during the child's day (for example, before eating, before going to bed) may be a useful support in case prayer should be forgotten or overlooked. Nonetheless, we should not give the child the impression that one is to pray only at certain times. We have already said how the person who lives constantly with the child may have many opportunities to pray with him. During the catechetical meetings, it is preferable, in our view, that prayer follow the catechist's presentation; in this way prayer takes the shape of a response to what has been proclaimed. Sometimes, if we feel the children to be so inclined, there may be a moment of prayer when everyone arrives at catechesis, or before they leave for home. On the other hand, there may be no such fixed times of prayer, remembering that listening is also prayer.

Celebrations

At times prayer will take the form of celebration in the true and real sense of the word, usually of two kinds: one that closely follows the Church's Liturgy, and the other extemporaneous in nature. In the first, we should be as faithful as possible to the liturgical structure, in such a way that these celebrations are not only an occasion for the children to pray, but also an occasion for their initiation into the living participation in the Liturgy. The Easter Liturgy is especially rich; we select the Liturgy of Light for the smaller children. To celebrate it we first darken all the rooms in the Center so that, as the children arrive, they will experience the disconcerting effect of the lack of light and so the resplendence of light in the Liturgy becomes more impressive and gratifying to them. The children themselves trace the cross, the *Alpha* and *Omega,* and the date of the year on the paschal candle; then they light it, carry it in procession, with the rest of the children following behind that single light that enables us to walk forward. Finally, the children light their own candles from the paschal candle, which is symbolic of the risen Christ. The celebration of light develops gradually as the children grow; later we add the passage of the "paschal proclamation" and the renewal of the baptismal promises. The moment when we linger to look at the light that has come all the way to us is often a time of intense contemplation, leaving a vivid memory that the growing children cherish. The children have in this way points of reference that will help them to orient themselves when they come to participate in the liturgy with the adult community.

We have already mentioned how the Christmas-Epiphany liturgical season, since it is less structured, may give rise to celebrations that are invented from time to time, which we call extemporaneous (cf. chapter 6). These serve to illuminate some moment in the community life of the children. In the cases when there is no structure, we need not create it. We should try to make the celebration adhere as closely as possible to what we want to celebrate, and try to make it an authentic expression of the feeling of that moment.

Since these celebrations must be a true expression of the children's community, they should not be restricted to only the younger children but should be lived by younger and older children together. The celebration will then structure itself according to the diversified contributions of both older and younger children: The more "manual" tasks are delegated to the younger children, for example, carrying the objects in procession and arranging them in their places; the older children choose and read the scriptural passages, begin the spontaneous prayer, and so forth. At times the initiative comes from the younger children, at other times from the older ones or the catechist; however, the catechist should confine himself or herself to launching the idea and offering some hints, leaving the children the task of seeking out the form that corresponds to their feelings. The catechist can help by posing some questions, such as what Gospel passages the children are considering reading (a parable? a narrative?); what songs they wish to choose; if they are thinking of staying in the atrium or if they would prefer to go to the church or chapel. If the children want to organize a procession, the catechist may ask questions about what is needed (what is to be carried? by whom?).

Photographs 15 and 16 show the development of a celebration directed by a group of children to solemnize their return to the Center after their first communion retreat. We outline the sequence decided by the children themselves on two such occasions as this:

Account of the Last Supper in the Eucharistic Prayer
Prayers of the final offering in the Eucharistic Prayer
Reading of the parable of the True Vine
Final hymn

Another time the children selected:

Reading of the Good Shepherd parable
Psalm 23 (Good Shepherd psalm)
Reading of the True Vine parable
Communion hymn

Photographs 17 and 18 show a group of children celebrating Pentecost. Seven candles are set out on a table in the prayer area; the children, after listening to the account of the descent of the Holy Spirit, write the names of the Spirit's gifts and place one beside each candle; then the children light their own candles from the candle that holds the name of the gift they would most like to have. The choice is always made with great seriousness, and often after long deliberation.

Silence

Finally, an essential element in the education to prayer is silence. We are not speaking about the silence during the moment

when one is praying; we are dealing with a real education to silence, which is not just the more or less imposed cessation of
noise but the silence that becomes something the child searches
for and loves, the silence in which the child feels totally at home.
Maria Montessori placed the importance of this in very clear relief; the "Silence Lesson," as it is called, is an extremely significant element in her schools. The children have shown that they
delight in the complete immobility that the lesson naturally involves and they rejoice in recollecting themselves in listening to
something that has no sound. Maria Montessori recounts how often it happened that when she began to write the word "silence"
on the board, the whole class stopped their work and became perfectly still before she had even finished writing the word. This is
a common phenomenon in Montessori schools. "I like everything
at catechesis," wrote Chiara, "but silence is the thing I like best."

We are not talking about that kind of empty silence which
can be obtained in every school, by raising one's voice perhaps,
especially when the children are restless. The silence we are
speaking of arises very slowly, through the control of even the
slightest movement, and extends to enfold the whole group of
children in some way. It does not enter from without; it is an interior silence, one that responds to the child's unspoken request
to be helped to be recollected. Therefore it should not be asked of
the children when we sense they are not disposed toward it; silence is not an aid for the teacher to bring the class to order; it is
a help to the meditative spirit of the child.

At times, when the silence is complete, we may eventually
suggest a line of a psalm in a low, solemn voice; but, in any event,
we should give the children a way to enjoy at length a silence
that is true and real. If silence is an essential element in Montessori schools, it is especially so in every center of catechesis. There
will not be the listening—that quality of listening the importance of which we have so often stressed—without the practice of
silence; there will not be prayer without silence.

We conclude by reiterating that every important point proclaimed during catechesis—if it is offered in an appropriate
form—will be transformed spontaneously into prayer. This takes
us back to the problem we touched on in chapter 4, that is, the
problem of controls in our work. We said there is no possibility of
an academic kind of control; it is impossible (and if it were possible, it would be irreverent) precisely because of the nature of the
content itself. Nevertheless, prayer can offer us a way of examin-

ing our work, in the sense that if the children's prayer is impoverished and empty it means the proclamation was not well given on our part: Perhaps the content itself was poor and did not relate to the exigencies of the children's age; maybe it was not proclaimed with a sufficiently religious spirit. Therefore the problem of controls, if we may speak of them at all, concerns our way of doing catechesis, and what should be refined is not the children's prayer but our own work.

NOTES

1. G. Milanesi, "Il pensiero magico nella preadolescenza," *Orientamenti pedagogici* (1967), 583.

Chapter Eight
Education to Wonder and the Kingdom of God

"The kingdom of God is like a mustard seed."
Matthew 13:31

It has been observed that "early childhood develops under the sign of wonder";[1] for the child everything is a source of wonder because everything is new. Wonder is an exceedingly important stimulus for the human spirit, so much so that Plato said: "This sense of wonder is the mark of the philosopher. Philosophy indeed has no other origin" (*Theaetetus,* 155 d). The UNESCO report on education states:

> Man's capacity for wonder is at the source of activities, such as the ability to observe, experiment and classify experience and information; to express himself and to listen, in the course of a discussion; to train his faculty for systematic doubt; to read—a never ending exercise; to question the world in ways combining the scientific and poetical frames of mind.[2]

If we were to better clarify the nature of the stimulus man receives from wonder, perhaps we could compare it to a magnet. The nature of wonder is not a force that pushes us passively from behind; it is situated ahead of us and attracts us with irresistible force toward the object of our astonishment; it makes us advance toward it, filled with enchantment.

Wonder is a dynamic value; nevertheless it does not drive us to activism but draws us to activity, to an activity we do as persons immersed in the contemplation of something that exceeds us. Maybe the particularity of wonder is that we find activity and contemplation inseparably blended within it.

I would like to elucidate right away that in speaking about wonder I do not intend to talk about something like *Alice in Wonderland.** Wonder is a very serious thing that, rather than leading us away from reality, can arise only from an attentive observation of reality. Education to wonder is correlative with an education that helps us to go always more deeply into reality. If we skim over things we will never be surprised by them. Wonder is not an emotion of superficial people; it strikes root only in the person whose mind is able to settle and rest in things, in the person who is capable of stopping and looking. It is only through a continued and profound observation of reality that we become conscious of its many aspects, of the secrets and mysteries it contains. Openness to reality and openness to wonder proceed at the same pace: As we gradually enter into what is real, our eyes will come to see it as more and more charged with marvels, and wonder will become a habit of our spirit.

All this is extremely important for education in the general sense, but it is perhaps especially so for religious education. When wonder becomes a fundamental attitude of our spirit it will confer a religious character to our whole life, because it makes us live with the consciousness of being plunged into an unfathomable and incommensurable reality. If we are disposed to reflect on reality in its complexity, then it will reveal itself to be full of the unexpected, of aspects we will never succeed in grasping or circumscribing; then we will be unable to close our eyes to the presence of something or someone within it that surpasses us. Even calling it "the absurd" is also a way of recognizing its immeasurability. But the religious person will break out in a hymn of praise and admiration.[3]

Wonder is proper to the child, poet, artist, and also to the old person who has known how to live by beholding and contemplat-

---

*Cavalletti is not just referring to the Walt Disney cartoon interpretation of Lewis Carroll's book. The editor of *The Annotated Alice,* Martin Gardner, gives full due to the seriousness of the laughter in this book that attracts serious and overly serious comment. To conclude his Introduction he paraphrases one of Reinhold Niebuhr's sermons to make the point that laughter only works on life's superficial absurdities but that it turns to bitterness and derision when it is directed toward the deeper irrationalities such as evil and death. Wonder is not irrelevant to these. (Lewis Carroll, *The Annotated Alice,* Introduction and Notes by Martin Gardner, New York: World Publishing Co., 1960.)

ing the world surrounding him in such a way that reality has revealed ever widening horizons to him. We can say that, according to their different levels of penetration, all is new to the child and the old person.

It is most important that this emotional capacity not be extinguished in the child. It has been remarked that one of the negative points of modern education is that it is "losing more and more the sense of surprise," and that "we are no longer amazed by anything." What can the adult do so that this most important feature will not be lost?

First of all, what the adult should *not do:* We should not give too many things, we should not offer too many stimuli. We should not alter too often or too rapidly the object of the child's attention, in which case the child would defend himself with an intentional indifference to this kind of wearying, continuous movie. If the child does not have the time to dwell on anything, then everything will come to seem the same to him and he will lose all interest in things. The Italian novelist Pavese observed: "We know that the surest—and quickest—way for us to wonder is to fix your gaze undauntedly on the same object. One fine moment this object will seem to us—miraculously—as if we have never seen it before."[4]

The child's wonder will be stifled by too much food, but also by food that is not nourishing. Wonder will be quenched if it does not find a worthy object, if it lingers on limited objects; such objects will inevitably disappoint the child. It is the educator's task, therefore, to offer the child's wonder an object capable of taking the child always farther and deeper into the awareness of reality, an object whose frontiers are always expanding as the child slowly proceeds in the contemplation of it.

The Mystery of the Kingdom of God

We believe that the Gospel offers us such an object, especially the parables of the Kingdom of God, which have enkindled that deep light in the children's eyes, a light we have seen time and time again. I intend to speak particularly about those parables that present the kingdom as an extremely small reality, which almost escapes our glance; nonetheless it is one that becomes, prodigiously, so great.

The Gospel invites us to contemplate the mystery of the kingdom in two different moments: the initial and concluding moments; these present us with the perturbing contrast of something very little and something very large. What is extraordinary is that the great comes from the small. The Gospel speaks to us of the mustard seed (Matthew 13:31–32), which is "the smallest of all seeds," great—as it is found in the land of Jesus, in Israel—but no bigger than the head of a pin; and yet it becomes a tree (*dendron*), to which the birds of the air come to make their nests. The Gospel speaks to us of a woman who mixes three measures of flour with yeast, until all the dough is leavened, transforming itself from a little mound of flour into a large loaf of bread (Matthew 13:33). No less astonishing is the story of that seed of grain the farmer sows in the ground: "It sprouts and grows, he knows not how. The earth produces of itself, first the blade, then the ear, and then the full grain in the ear" (Mark 4:26–29).

All three parables manifest the two extreme moments of a process without pausing over the development, thereby stressing the contrast between the small and the great, and the great that comes from the small. Indeed, the growth of life is so marvelous that we cannot catch hold of it during its process, yet it inspires our attention when it is already accomplished in some way. No one has ever seen grass growing, or a flower bloom, but everyone has experienced the surprise at the transformation, which seems so sudden to us, of a field that loses its winter look to put on once again the face of spring, or at the first appearance of a bud on a branch that the day before appeared dry and withered. These parables help us to rest in this state of spirit—but not to stop there. The little seed, the leaven, becomes the springboard to reach the deepest level of reality, in order to glean its universal meaning: With these little elements as a point of departure, we see the same wonderful activity taking place throughout the whole world. There is a force working within the entire universe that constantly exceeds its premises. It is the secret of creation: from an immeasurable littleness to the greatest of realities by means of an energy that surpasses every human capacity. That vital breath which swells the small mustard seed and makes it become a great tree is the breath within all that is created, and it calls man forth into a marvelous movement that goes, incredibly, from the less to the more.

Starting with the consideration of that small seed, which gets lost in the palm of our hand, the world surrounding us becomes transparent little by little, and we catch sight of an extraordinary force at work there, which is also ours in some way because we perceive its action within ourselves, yet at the same time it totally surpasses us. There is in these parables—which do not speak explicitly of God—a silent and most apparent presence of God, because they place us face to face with a reality in which man is involved, by which he is somehow carried, and at the same time it eludes him. How great is the wonder and joy in discovering ourselves to be part of such a mystery.

When we say "parable" we are indicating a certain method of teaching (cf. chapter 10), a certain literary genre, which however has different forms. We could define the parables we have mentioned as "revelatory parables"; they really reveal to us the secret of the universe and lead us to contemplate it. Perhaps this is why the child, the "metaphysical and contemplative" child, receives them with such ease and such silent recollection. They offer an element of ever-growing reflection; with these there is not the danger that the child will soon come up against a limit that arrests his meditation and extinguishes his wonder.

In our view, these parables are the means with which to initiate the child into the mystery of life. Nowadays there is great concern, and with reason, about the need to educate the person to a religious reading of reality, to an understanding of "creation signs." But this reading should begin at the right age and at the right time. If early childhood is the right age, as we believe it is, then the level should be metaphysical and the approach global. The task of the educator of young children, it seems to us, is not to assist the child to distinguish this or that element of reality. The educator's work is far greater: It is a matter of helping the child to contemplate the miracle of Life in itself. The enjoyment, the "falling in love" the child is capable of in relation to God, should be expanded to embrace everything in which His Spirit is present and manifests Himself, persons and things; in everything we call, to use the biblical term, the "Kingdom of God." It is against this background of global love for life that every manifestation of life, in persons and things, comes to be colored with love.

However, we cannot love life's details if life as such has not become visible to us as a mysterious gift that enfolds and penetrates us. Reading the details will be done by the older child when his eyes, which as a child were fixed in the profound scrutiny of reality, now open toward the expanded horizon surrounding him and the many aspects it holds. But the older child must not come to this moment unprepared. If in early childhood he has received the religious content of reality in its wholeness, then it will be possible in later childhood to read its details in a religious key as well. Reality enlarges itself before the older child, yet it also becomes more fragmentary, and so it is necessary that the child face it carrying within himself a global vision. Helping the child to read this or that sign of creation can become a superficial, sterile work if the older child does not already have within himself a key with which to interpret it. It seems to us that the movement of the spirit is from the center to the periphery, from the essential to the secondary, from the global to the particular.[5] Without adequate preparation, reading the details may easily become something that is done only on the part of the adult and does not arise from the heart of the older child himself.

As a matter of fact, too often we become preoccupied with the details without first giving the whole. We guide the child to find the imprint of God's presence in this or that person or in this or that event, but we do not give sufficient care to initiate the child into the contemplation of the miracle of Life in itself. We think this is due to the fact that early childhood, the period when one's "hold" on reality is global, is disregarded; and once more the educational work that has neglected early childhood presents itself as founded on a void.

The very form of the parables we cited promotes wisdom. The child's attention is called to something that has a twofold attraction: its littleness—the child's capacity for discovering the smallest things and considering them with great concentration is well known—and the contrast it offers when juxtaposed with something very great. This should be the pivotal point of the meditation that follows the presentation of the text. In this first point there is already ample material for meditation: "What extraordinary energy there must be to transform the little seed into a tree, or into a full ear of grain, or a small handful of flour and water into a swollen lump of dough! Would we know how to do it ourselves? Is there any person who can do such a thing? We can make big things too, but only by putting many small things together. But the tree is not the sum of many seeds, it is the growth of *one* seed! Where does such mysterious energy come from?"

This is just the beginning of our meditation; we must then widen the circle: "The marvel we see in the little mustard seed takes place in all the seeds of this world. When we see a tall tree it seems impossible to us that it could come from a small seed; and yet it is so! And this happens in fields all over the world. What a mysterious and powerful energy must envelop the world so that this may happen! And maybe we see it very close to us?"

Now we help the children to recognize the same prodigious energy in themselves: "We were so small when we were born! Now look at us! Touch yourselves: How tall are we? How long are our arms, our legs? Is it due to us? If I wanted to be taller or shorter, could I do it? Then this force that makes me grow, is it mine or not? Is it a gift we receive? From whom? Even more important: Once we did not know how to talk or walk, and now, how many things do we know how to do! We too have been transformed and are being transformed in our bodies, and within us. We have grown and we are growing—wonderfully—from a less to a more. While the growth of our body reaches a certain point and stops, inside us there is a capacity to become 'greater' that continues for our whole life. ('A kingdom inside us!' exclaimed Linda with enchantment.) Our whole life is to make real this kingdom within us, up to and beyond death. Death is nothing more than a new, more important passage from a less to a more."

In our estimation these parables, which initiate the child into the mystery of life, can also be a way to initiate the child to the mystery of death, understood as the moment of the transformation of life itself; we are living as persons immersed in the great reality of life, and even death is a passage toward a "more," toward a better. Nevertheless, we should keep in mind that early childhood is not the time to ponder the fact that the little seed must die in order to bear fruit, that the less becomes the more on the condition that it pass through death. This is a separate element, and the greater the realities the more they should be given one at a time. With young children we should focus on the fact that death does not stop the movement of life toward the more, not on *how* this happens.

Finally, there is another aspect of great importance that these parables help to illuminate: the religious sense of our bodies. As we have said, these parables provide us with a way to help the child meditate on his own physical growth and on the fact that the transformation he is able to witness in his body happens within him, but it is not his own; the child is not the master of his body nor can he adjust it to suit his own pleasure. In man, as within all creation, there is a force that eludes us and that we will never be able to give to ourselves; if we see it at work within our bodies this happens because it has been given to us as a gift.

An affirmation like this helps the child to regard his body with a sense of wondrous admiration and to make it the object of deep respect. The body, no less than the seed, becomes a sign of the mystery, and can be a sign because it is itself a bearer of the mystery. Every part of the body, without losing any of its concreteness, is colored with the light of the Infinite, and we discover a new dignity in our bodies.

In other words, these parables are a valuable instrument for sexual education as well.[6] We think the catechist has a specific task in this sphere. Berge affirms that it is the family's role to introduce the child to the mysteries of sexuality with that affective warmth which only parents can give to the subject;[7] then there is the school, whose task is primarily informative; yet there is a third aspect of sexuality: the religious dimension. There are wonderful mechanisms in our bodies; our birth is linked to an act of love that binds two persons together and makes them bearers of life. All this is truly beautiful and important; but we should go even further, to the origin of all this: to the living God who gives us life, who cares for and conserves life.

In our view, this is the particularity of the catechist's task in matters related to sexual education, which is nothing other than an aspect of moral education (cf. chapter 9). Once again, it is the task of the catechist of young children to take things down to their deepest roots.

The Value of the Kingdom of God

We present two other parables to the young children to integrate those we have already spoken about: the parable of the merchant who goes in search of precious pearls and when he has found one of great value, sells all that he has to buy it (Matthew 13:45–46); and the parable of the man who, digging in a field, finds a "hidden treasure" and "in his joy" he too sells all that he has to buy that field (Matthew 13:44). These two parables lead to contemplation and action at the same time. There is a strong ascetic factor in that both protagonists renounce all they have. However, this is not the aspect that strikes the young children and we should be careful not to highlight it with them; it is an element that relates to the interior attitude of the adolescent, or at the earliest, of the preadolescent.

In the younger children, these two parables also stimulate contemplation exclusively and reinforce what the other three parables have helped them to consider: so great is the value of that kingdom which is inside us and around us that it surpasses every other thing. Attention should be centered on the pearl of great value—how beautiful it must be!—and on the hidden treasure—containing who knows how many precious gems!—and *not* on what man must do to have them. The child is not yet at the age when he must "do." The proclamation is given to the child not to direct him in the immediate present to some moral realization, but, according to the words of Bultmann cited earlier, for the "completion of being," which will be manifested only at a later time through a certain way of living. Once more, yet in a different manner, these parables make us stop to marvel at the kingdom and the great happiness there is in belonging to it. It seems to us that these parables, because of the opportunities they present to be applied to ever-expanding spaces of reality, can offer an object of meditation that will not disappoint the child, a food worthy of the child's wonder.

The presentation of these parables follows the same sequence described in chapter 3, namely: narration of the parable, initiation into the meditation on it, solemn reading of the Gospel text. The materials for the children's personal work on the parables of the mustard seed, leaven, and grain of wheat are the small Gospel booklets, one for each parable; if the children can write they love to copy the text, or they may illustrate it. In relation to these parables, there is no real material for the children's work, as there is for the Good Shepherd parable for instance; the "material" for these parables is the world, including our own bodies. These parables have such a particular scope that they do not allow themselves to be enclosed with a material, in the technical sense of the word. However, the children may plant seeds and watch their growth. For the leaven parable, we prepare two different batches of dough with the children, putting only flour and water in one, and adding yeast to the other. After the dough is covered, it is only at the end of the two-hour meeting that the children uncover them to discover the difference between them, a difference that depends solely on the leaven's force. The force of the yeast is such that it changes not only the volume of the dough, but also the color, taste, texture, and odor.

There is a sequence of action in the parable of the merchant and the pearl: following the Gospel reading we present the materials through which we concretize these movements, then the materials are left for the children to use. We have built a wooden environment that represents the merchant's house. We move the figure of the merchant in and out of the house while he is shown to be amassing many boxes filled with pearls; after the last journey, when the merchant finds the pearl of great value, he disposes of his many pearls and only one is left in his house: the pearl of great value.

The Responsiveness in the Children

The following is an excerpt from a catechist's unpublished diary from Borgata Casilina, Rome. It records the observations of a group of six-year-old children on the parable of the merchant:

—Who could have made the merchant understand that
the pearl was worth more than all the others?
—The Holy Spirit.
—The merchant wasn't a prophet, but still he listened to
Him.
—He gave away all the pearls, except the one that was
real, the others were false. Then he was happy.
—He doesn't show anyone, he closed the door because they
were disturbing him.

(Twice I have done this parable with different groups of
children, and always when I moved the figure of the
merchant to return home with the pearl of great price,
the children shouted: "Close the door!" whereas I had
left it open so they could see inside better!)[8]

—It sure wasn't the sun that gave that light to the pearl,
God did, and that's why it wasn't seen.
—It's great, the robbers don't see, so they can't take it
away.
—If you compare it to the sun, the pearl wins.
—If the sun and pearl were together, who knows what a
beautiful day that would be!
—With wax the floors become bright, they shine. But with
the pearl, the whole house shines.

—But where is the pearl?
—In the heart! Who knows how it glows!

The following conversation on the parable of the leaven is taken from the same diary:

—The leaven has God's strength because only He can make it grow.
—The leaven is the kingdom of God.
—How big can it get?
—It can go as high as the sky because the Kingdom of God is great.
—It never stops growing.
—It's in our hearts.

(After seeing the dough rise, the wonder and joy reached a peak.)

—Beautiful! It's true! Jesus was right! Jesus tells the truth.
—It's so big!
—God must have given the force to the leaven.
—Jesus was speaking about His kingdom.
—His kingdom must grow and we believe it because He can't tell lies.
—It must grow up to the sky; it will never stop growing because Jesus is powerful.
—We are thinking of the kingdom of God.
—It's in heaven, but the place He likes best is the heart.
—It's a powerful kingdom.
—Jesus gives us the pearl of great price, the treasure, the powerful kingdom, and we are happy.
—Other gifts don't matter to us, because we have the gift of Jesus, Who is more beautiful and powerful.

The fact worth noting in the following section is that when the catechist wanted to begin a discussion on Easter, the children's responses were in reference to the parables:

—Easter is coming, the greatest feast. What can we do to prepare ourselves?

—Think of the pearl, the treasure . . . the leaven.

—When is the feast?

—When the leaven has grown and made all the dough grow.

—The merchant—when he is happy?

—When he has the pearl that is worth more than all the others.

—Now we must have a party for Jesus with candles, because they have light.

—The more you love God the happier you are.

—A little girl should listen to the Holy Spirit. The more she listens the more light Jesus gives her.

—The Holy Spirit is like fire: He gives light and warmth.

—He makes you understand the secrets of God and says them to you one by one.

—But you hear them with your heart, where the pearl is.

—He speaks in a whisper.

Drawing number 48 shows that children know how to interiorize the content of the parables: The treasure is in the heart. The creativity with which the child relates the parables to other elements is remarkable in drawings 49 and 50. With regard to significant drawings like these, we quote a passage from a past student's letter:

Rochester, New York
December 3, 1976

Dear Sofia,

When I saw the drawings your children had done I thought mine would never be able to do such profound work. Instead, I was really amazed to see some of their drawings on the kingdom of God and the pearl. A six-year-old boy did a drawing of Christ and he put the pearl in Jesus' hand. Another boy drew a large cross, and in the center he put a pearl. Another boy made a sort of book which he called the "Book of God" and put the pearl on the cover. And what surprised me even more is that none of this entered into our conversation on the parable. . . ."

NOTES

1. G. Durand, *L'imagination symbolique* (Paris: PUF, 1968), p. 80.

2. AA.VV. *Learning to Be* (Paris: UNESCO Press, 1972), p. 155.

3. G. von Rad, *Israël et la sagesse* (Génève: Labor et Fides, 1970), pp. 190, 339ff. German Edition, *Weisheit in Israel* (Neukirchen-Vluyn, 1970).

4. C. Pavese, *I dialoghi con Leucò* (Milano: Mondadori, 1972), p. 33.

5. P. Ricoeur, *Finitude et culpabilité* (Paris: Aubier-Montaigne, 1960), *Vol. I,* p. 24.

6. *To Teach As Jesus Did:* A Pastoral Message on Catholic Education. National Conference of Catholic Bishops (Washington: United States Catholic Conference, November 1972).

7. A. Berge, *Education sexuelle chez l'enfant* (Paris: PUF, 1970).

8. The children are likely referring to the Gospel maxim: "But when you pray, go into your room and shut the door and pray to your Father who is in secret" (Matthew 6:6).

Chapter Nine
Moral Formation*

"God is love."
(1 John 4:8)

It may appear out of place to talk about moral formation in a book dealing with children from three to six years of age, that is, the age preceding the time when the child begins to become interested explicitly in behavior. It is well known that the child under the age of six is not interested in moral behavior as such; thus he is unable to receive moral formation, understood in this sense. If we tried to give the child a direct moral formation we would have the same result as a nursery school teacher who wanted to tell the children about the parable of the prodigal son; the children's only reaction to this parable was the question: "What happened to those pigs?" The teacher drew the conclusion that parables are not suited to young children, whereas it was the choice of parable that was at fault. The children responded in the only way appropriate to their age: Since they are in the sensitive period for protection, they were struck only by the fact that the swine were left abandoned, and the whole problematic of sin and conversion completely escaped them.

Nevertheless, morality does not concern only actions. By morality we mean above all a certain orientation of the whole person in life, the leaning forward of the being toward a point; we could compare this to heliotropism, that movement whereby plants turn toward the sun. The multiplicity of actions arise from this one, fundamental orientation, which involves the

---

*The examples given in this chapter concern children over the age of six, because it is after this age that the motivations of behavior become explicit.

whole person. The relation between orientation and actions is like a plant and its fruits; there are living fruits only if the plant is healthy and rooted deeply in the earth. Actions are the manifold expressions of the global orientation of the person.

This fundamental orientation should already be established by the time the older child begins to ask his first questions in regard to the value of individual actions. We would like to repeat here what we said in the preceding chapter: Before the older child comes to consider the details of reality, he should first be helped to find a universal key that allows him to approach these details in the right way. Before the older child begins to question himself whether this or that action is good or bad, we should have provided him with a "yardstick" with which he can give his own response when the time comes; we should give the older child a reference point to orient himself in the new horizon that is opening before him. The yardstick must already be prepared by the time he needs it. The adult's hurried intervention in the moment when the moral crisis is already in action is undoubtedly detrimental. The older child will either rebel against an inopportune intrusion, or he will become accustomed to using someone else's yardstick; then morality will not be the child's own listening to the voice of the Spirit, but rather obedience to an external law. Thus the older child—and often the adult as well—will stay on a level of moral immaturity.

Maria Montessori speaks of a series of "planes of development" in the life of the person; each one can be harmoniously constructed only if the preceding planes have been well established. The moral plane, in the sense of interest in behavior, coincides with later childhood; the older child will be able to face it without trauma only if he has lived his early childhood in a certain way.

The Enjoyment of God and the Moral Life

In early childhood the child's fundamental need is to be loved with a protective love, and to have someone to love; it is on the foundation of the satisfaction of this exigence that one can base the moral life of the older child. We have seen that the religious experience, the enjoyment of God's presence in our life, has a fundamental part in the satisfaction of this exigence, so much so that we can say that every religious experience and any kind of religious formation in early childhood contribute to the child's harmonious formation in the present, and they are an *indirect moral preparation* for later childhood. In fact, what is morality in the Christian view if not the response to God's love, our reaction to our encounter with Him? Therefore the adult who wants to give children a moral formation should refrain from any promptings of the common kind in the moral order; instead the adult should announce God's love and help the child to experience and enjoy it in reflection and prayer. We believe that the more profound, deeply felt, and enjoyed the child's religious experience is, the more ready, autonomous, and genuine will be the response of the older child.

We would like to underline "genuine," because if the child has become conscious of a certain reality, if the child has in some way experienced, enjoyed, and *fallen in love* with it, then this reality will reflower in later childhood, and the first moral uneasiness of this period will be colored with its light, which is the light of love.

Over the years we have been able to observe consistently how some subjects that were presented to the younger child, without any moral allusion, become reference points for the new experience the older child is living. The young child has "seen" the gift of God in the baptismal signs and has been enraptured by it. The parables of the kingdom we have spoken about revealed to the young child how mysterious and of what great value this gift is, and in listening to the parables the child's eyes were opened wide, filled with wonder and enchantment. Then, when the older child comes to make an examination of conscience, for him it is to "look and see if there are any marks on the baptismal gown," it is to "see if the Kingdom of God is inside us." These are expressions that are often heard from children around the ages of seven and eight.

"The Shepherd would not have brought his sheep back to the fold by force," a catechist remarked; Eugenio (seven years old) reflected: "The sheep must have thought of the Kingdom of God he had lost, and how beautiful it was." A boy told Paolo (eight years old) that he had told his mother a lie, and Paolo responded: "But you've marked your baptismal gown." "What do you think of," a catechist asked, "when you see a person going to confession?" Tomasso (seven and a half years old) replied: "That he is taking care of his white gown"; another boy (nine years old) answered: "That he wants the gift of a cleaner baptismal gown."

The realities that captivated the younger child are reactivated to inform the older child's new plane of development, which is concerned with moral questions. In this fact we witness the guarantee that the proclamation and catechesis offered in the preceding years have truly constituted a vital event for the child. The child's contemplation of the gratifying reality of God's protective love has not been sterile in his life; so profound has been its effect that the child, *years later,* spontaneously refers to it. The reality has become so much a part of the child's person that now he can apply it in a different context. The child has not only been cradled in the certainty of being loved; the child has received a seed capable of bearing immediate and long-term fruit.

To us it seems of great importance that the older child lives his first problems of behavior in the light of a loved and enjoyed reality. In this way when the older child begins to become aware of his deficiencies, the sorrow he feels will flow from the best source: from the love of a great gift that has been received. Falling in love is the "plane of development" on which the older child's life is founded, and it is only in love, and not in fear, that one may have a moral life worthy of the name. The older child will not be a slave who abstains from doing certain things for fear of punishment, but he will be a person who is free and empowered by love.

The same vision of the Good Shepherd's love expands: It is no longer only a love in which the Shepherd gives Himself, but a love that is capable of forgiving as well. The enjoyment the child experienced in considering the Good Shepherd's love now grows into the deep joy of knowing himself to be loved and supported, even if one is an imperfect sheep; that the Good Shepherd's love does not stop when faced with deficiency whatever it may be, and that it surpasses every human capacity. Paola (eight years old) observed: "When I get lost at the supermarket Mommy yells at me; the Good Shepherd isn't like that, He doesn't yell at the sheep when He finds it."

In the presence of the proclamation of the Good Shepherd's unfailing love, we have seen the older children become enraptured, and enjoy with that same quality of profound inner enjoyment which the younger children manifest in their first meeting with the Good Shepherd.

The initial moment of the moral crisis can be a time of perplexity and loss for the older child who is not sustained, in this period as well, by the certainty of being loved despite his every incapacity and inadequacy. Nevertheless, this certainty cannot be improvised. It is the same certitude as that of the young child, yet lived in a different existential situation; it is the same certitude as that of the young child, which has grown with him; it is the certitude that the young child has lived in the serene peace of his early childhood and that the older child now refinds and develops with the amplitude of a different horizon. But for this to happen the older child must have lived it in early childhood.

The Importance of Early Childhood

Therefore, it is from the point of view of moral formation as well that the religious experience before six years of age seems so important to us. Before this age, the relationship with God is established without contrasts; the child is free from any preoccupation and open to the encounter with God and to the enjoyment he derives from it. To coincide the beginning of catechesis, or religious formation of whatever kind, with the age when the older child is opening up to moral values can have, in our estimation, serious consequences. The meeting with God is confused with moral problems, and God will easily come to assume the aspect of judge.

"There are many human lives," observes Arago-Mitjans, "that exclude God *precisely* because of the untimely influence of religiousness on morality."[1] We wonder if the fact that God is primarily a judge for so many people is not due to the general custom of coinciding religious practice and the beginning of catechesis with the start of the period of moral interests. The necessity of catechesis, or in any case some religious formation, before the age of six finds its most valid reason in this fact. In our view, catechesis that is started around six to seven years of age can confuse the face of God for the child.

On the other hand, the importance of the prescholastic period is stressed by the whole of modern psychology. The UNESCO report on education, which we have already cited,[2] speaks of the "social crime" that is committed in leaving unutilized the child's numerous potentialities. Should not a similar cry of alarm be raised in the religious sphere as well? There are many scholars who have experienced personally what the child is capable of before six years of age; for instance, the impressive experience recounted by Doman in his book *How to Teach Your Baby to Read*,[3] as one example among many. Some countries, realizing this to be the case, have organized vast preschool educational systems; in first place are China and the U.S.S.R. The latter receives almost ten million children into its nurseries and day-care centers.[4]

What can be done in the catechetical field with children under six years of age? In Italy a catechism for young children has been issued; it has, however, great lacunae; innovations for the very young child are extremely scarce. It is true that in early childhood the task of religious formation concerns the parents primarily, but "primarily" does not mean "exclusively." The catechist's work is not complete without the parents' contribution, but the reverse is also true. We are dealing with two different ways, which are complementary and not alternatives.

Furthermore, the number of children spending the major part of the day in nurseries and day-care centers is always increasing. What are we doing for them? Do not the affirmations regarding the great potentialities of early childhood hold true in the religious realm as well? We ask ourselves if the adult's sensitivity is sufficiently awakened to this immense problem, or if we are not culpable in letting the age pass by when, more than at any other age, the child asks us for religious food and we leave him to a total fast.

In starting catechesis at six years of age, or even later, we unavoidably confuse, as we said, the religious plane with the plane of morality, as regards behavior; we also coincide the initiation into the Christian message with the time when the child begins to have greater intellectual needs. Then catechesis must necessarily conform itself to these needs without, however, being based on the affective richness proper to the preceding age. Therefore, there will be no possibility of that affective integration which gives warmth to what is received and which, in a just equilibrium with intellectual perception, will ensure a profound effect on one's life. Catechesis will be grasped more by the child's mind than with his heart ("heart" understood in the biblical sense, meaning the synthesis of the capacities of the whole person). Catechesis will easily become one among the many academic subjects.

It seems to us that the child's very structure—contemplative in early childhood, directed to moral interests realized in actions and more marked intellectual needs in later childhood—renders urgent the problem of the religious formation of young children. "We must reach early childhood at any cost," Tilmann states, "that is, the period up to six years of age."[5]

NOTES

1. Arago-Mitjans, *op. cit.*, p. 307.
2. *Learning to Be,* p. 108.
3. G. Doman, *How to Teach Your Baby to Read* (New York: Random House, 1964). Italian Edition, *Leggere a tre anni* (Roma: Armando, 1970).
4. *Learning to Be,* pp. 190–191.
5. Dreher, Exeler and Tilmann, *La sterilità della catechesi infantile* (Modena: Paoline, 1969), p. 26.

Chapter Ten
The Method of Signs

"On the subject of divine things, he who believes
he has already found does not find what
he is looking for, and has searched in vain."
Saint Leo the Great

In our estimation, the choice of method is related to the question of content. There are certain contents that cannot be communicated except by certain methodologies. The method is not like an empty box that can be filled with anything whatsoever; the method has a soul, and this soul should correlate to the content that is being transmitted through the method. Between method and content there should be a profound accord, an affinity of nature; otherwise there is the risk of distorting the content.

Theology came to assume a methodological direction that was abstract and intellectualistic in character (the first foreshadowings arose during the late Middle Ages) and catechesis became the transmission of propositions already solved and enunciated in synthetic form; there was nothing left for the person to do but to receive them as they were, without committing oneself on a personal level beyond the effort to memorize. Having abandoned the language of images used by the great Church Fathers, catechesis fell into "formula-ism." It has been observed that when theology ceases to speak through images, it loses its hold on people and becomes a science of the specialists.[1]

But can theology, in the strong sense of the word, be reserved for the elect few, from an intellectual point of view? On the subject of "formula-ism," Alonso-Schoekel has observed:

The difficulty does not come from the fact, let us note, that the formulation is erroneous; it resides in the very fact of the use of formula. We should not complain to ourselves that the reasoning is poorly constructed or that it must be improved, but rather that the pedagogical preoccupation with formula tends to restrict and distort the Scriptural text.[2]

Actually such a distortion could not be otherwise; it gives rise to a great misunderstanding, because the mystery one is trying to convey is not definable, and thus a dangerous confusion cannot help but be created in the mind of the person to whom we wish to communicate the mystery. The Africans in a village in Chad, who were used to the old-style catechism, remarked to the catechist who presented the parables to them: "With you everything is different, it is not just a matter of learning."

All this has caused a reaction that has transformed the theologian into a "listener and interpreter," a reaction that obviously has had its influence on catechesis. As we said earlier, the catechist and child are both "listeners" to an unfathomable Word that unfolds itself as always new before their astonished eyes; Saint Gregory the Great says of Scripture: "In that certain way it grows with its readers; the uneducated recognize it, the educated find it always new."[3]

Therefore the method we use should be one that does not enclose or restrict, one that does not give the impression that everything has already been researched and resolved and that nothing remains for the individual to do.[4] It cannot be other than a method that is allusive in character, that offers itself without pretense, in the conviction that in the presence of God's Word—which surpasses man as "heaven surpasses the earth"—we can only provide some hints, some peripheral tools, that will help each "listener" to go slowly toward the center. A method such as this, even if it is excluded from the scholastic classrooms and consequently from catechesis, has however always remained alive where the life of the Church is living, and that is in the Liturgy.

Signs, The Method of the Church

The Liturgy has always spoken through "signs";[5] and Jesus taught only "in parables" (Mark 4:34). Biblical religion is the religion of the unknowable and transcendent God, Who reveals Himself; this apparent contradiction is resolved in the sign. It has been said that a sign is "a thing which indicates another thing different from itself"; Saint Augustine said of the sign: "You see one thing, you understand another from it." This is so, not because of an ambiguity of logic or an incapacity for clarity, but because of the sign's richness of meaning and ability to open ever wider horizons of the real.

The transcendent is manifested in the sign through a language that is primarily visual, and as such it is immediate, involving the whole person in one's totality, preventing any evasion into the abstract; the sign connects us to the sensible world while it urges us to reach toward the Invisible. Man's perceptive capacity is enlarged and deepened and he becomes capable of seeing beyond the appearances; in the sign the material world acquires a kind of transparency and the transcendent world a kind of tangibility.

There are signs that are more specifically religious, such as the biblical and liturgical signs. We have described our use of signs in catechesis: The essential doctrine of the Mass and Baptism are presented by means of the signs that constitute their rites; the light, the gestures, are sensible elements whose meaning is not exhausted in what we see; signs in some way make visible to us the great invisible reality of the gift of God. The signs point out to us the unfathomable reality of the Kingdom of God through little things; elements from everyday life (bread, wine, water, etc.), and in this way they propose to us an object of meditation that can be continuous, and at the same time they show us how little things can have a great range. The sign is a poverty that holds great richness and continues in itself the "scandal of the Incarnation."[6]

Parables as Signs

The parable has a special position among the biblical signs. The parable is a sign inasmuch as it is composed of words; however, its character as word is not to make explicit but rather to hide and veil, making it in some sense a sign twice over. Paraphrasing Saint Augustine, we could say of the sign: "You sense one thing, you understand another from it"; the difference between parable and sign is only in the sense through which we perceive the one and the other, but the methodology is the same.

The parable is a method of teaching; we can even say it is *the* method of the teaching of Jesus. The secret of the parable resides in its concealing what it wants to teach; the parable does not explain, clarify, or "define"; it offers an element for meditation. Saint Jerome, in speaking about parables, adopts the image of a nut enclosed in its shell; we could also add the image of a jewel encased in a box, wrapped in many layers of paper; we are not able to get at the savory or precious contents right away. In the parables there is a sort of facade behind which is hidden a house with many rooms; we must enter there slowly, with light tread, with veneration.

Like the sign, the parable alludes therefore to a different reality. In the Gospel there are various kinds of parables, which have different didactic intentions and hence different structures as well. Some, which we have dealt with briefly in this book, we have defined as "revelatory parables"; in these we find the two extreme levels of reality aligned side by side: the Kingdom of Heaven is like a woman making bread. From such an unexpected combination, a spark is emitted that begins to illuminate the darkness and to entice us to search diligently within the parables to the reality beyond. The greater the diversity between the two elements, the greater the "linguistic event" will be, and thus the stronger the impression we will receive from it and the more compelling the urge toward our own search. A linguistic event such as this is not a literary expedient in which two terms are unexpectedly juxtaposed for the purpose of impressing the reader, but rather the spark that results from such an event is something that was not known before: It is the revelation of a hidden reality.

In order to pierce the meaning of the parable we need to work with our imagination and our intuition. We need to use our imagination because we must not move away from the images through which the parable reveals reality to us. The author of the parable has not worked with fantasy; the likeness he is suggesting to us between the two levels of reality is not his own personal creation, nor is it a literary contrivance; it is an ontological likeness: The Kingdom of God can be compared to a mustard seed because the seed *is* in some way a bearer of the reality of the kingdom. Parables, or at least some of them, as we have said, are revelatory of reality. The two elements from which they more or less derive serve as our guide, almost as if they were two tracks along which our meditation should progress, in order to keep us from giving free reign to our fantasy. In doing a patient work of "mining" the most simple element of the parable, we will gradually reach the other pole. However, we also need to use our intuition at the same time, because the levels the parable juxtaposes are incommensurable, and we cannot catch hold of the relationship between them except through intuition. The parables indeed share in the nature of poetry;[7] for this reason they cannot be translated; in the sense that the images of which they are composed cannot be changed, they cannot even be explained.

If the particularity of the parable is that it only alludes to what it wants to teach, and to do so with the aim of giving space to our own personal search, then to explain the parable would mean killing it, destroying its most profound didactic wisdom. Teaching parables by explaining them would be tantamount to teaching through definitions. Jeremias has demonstrated that the two Gospel passages explaining the parables (Matthew 13:18–23, 36–42) do not date back to the original stratum of the text and therefore they are not the words of Jesus.[8] To explain the parables means to fasten them in a given interpretation, to suffocate their inexhaustible vitality; it means preventing the possibility of the listener's own personal discovery. To explain the parables is like fixing a butterfly on a pin; the wings are there still but the butterfly can no longer fly.

Faced with the ease with which the children let themselves be taken into the parables and faced with the difficulty of modern man in understanding biblical language, we ask ourselves, with Alonso-Schoekel, if this difficulty is not due to the fact that such language is "old, antiquated, impossible, or rather to the fact that we elevate ourselves in front of it in our pride. . . . Perhaps biblical language is the language of the poor in spirit."[9]

Creation Signs

Modern man is especially sensitive to what we used to call "creation signs"; it is not only the Bible and Liturgy that speak of God, but the whole of reality and every creature within it. Today our interest converges primarily on man. Schillebeeckx observes that in a cosmocentric vision, man's attention is centered especially on material things: water, balsam, images; in an anthropocentric world such as ours, man's attention is turned by preference toward the "ethical sign," and therefore to man.[10]

The parables of the kingdom, which we spoke about in chapter 8, are an instrument with which to initiate the person into the reading of the creation signs, for they are revelatory of a secret of the universe concerning man and things. As to the reading of the sign of "man" in particular, the parable of the Good Shepherd proves once again to be of greatest importance. Signs and parables, as we have said, are composed of two elements, which we could also call the departure point (for example, the mustard seed) and the point of arrival (in this case, the Kingdom of God); what the "reader" of the sign or parable must do is to establish the relation between these two poles. When we present the Good Shepherd parable to children, we proclaim Christ's protective love to them; and then, as we have seen, it is the child himself who, having experienced the love of mother, father, brothers, sisters, friends, "reads" this love in reference to the Good Shepherd. In this case one of the poles of the sign is provided by catechesis, the other by experience. The child not only searches for the link existing between the two poles, but he finds himself to be of these two poles, seeing in the lesser the reflection of the greater. The child reads in a Christological key the ethical sign of the love he experiences.

The Education to the Reading of Signs

With regard to this subject, we should remember that neither language nor—even less so—the reading of it is an instinctive function. Even Galileo stated that "the book of the universe is open to all, but in order to understand one needs to know its language and the letters in which it is written; it is written in mathematical language," and that is, in signs. The book of the universe can remain silent to the person who has not been initiated into its language, to the one who has not been trained to know its signs, that is, to read beyond appearances. Indeed, language "is not an instinctive, but an acquired 'cultural' function," observes E. Sapir.[11] This is true for signs as well.

The child should be initiated into the language of signs. The child is faced with something that signifies more than itself (*"significante"*), for instance, a person he loves, a mustard seed; but for the child to be able to read this in its profundity, it is necessary to help him know the other pole, without which the sign does not exist. Without such help, the thing that signifies can remain mute and opaque, precisely because the sign—composed of something that signifies (*"significante"*) and something that is signified (*"significato"*) inseparably united[12]—is not formed, and thus there is obviously no possibility of reading it. The universe can remain flat, without perspective. For the sign to become animated, to speak, and to acquire depth, it is necessary to indicate a point on the horizon to which to refer oneself. It is the presence of these two poles that gives birth to that "tension," of which Ricoeur speaks,[13] which arouses a "creation of sense," thereby conferring a dynamism to the sign that is not found in either one of the two components alone. If God's love is not proclaimed to the child, how could the child relate it to the love he experiences in those persons who are dear to him? The kerygma is therefore the essential point of departure.

In implementing the method of signs in our presentation of the kerygma we are making use of an allusive method, as we said; we give the child an instrument that is peripheral, so to speak, leaving to the child the work of reaching the vital nucleus through an activity that involves him personally and wholly. The child will constantly return to the facts we have provided him, making them an ever new object of his meditation in his dialogue with the interior Master, and he will reach a high degree of penetration into the parables. We could illustrate the first moment in the following way:

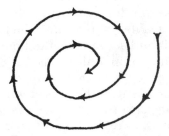

Once having arrived at this point, the work is not yet finished and the sign has not yet completed its task. Now the sign becomes an instrument—once again indispensable—of an activity that will lead the child to enter always more deeply into what has been proposed. Slowly, as we go deeper into the heart of things by concentrating on one point, we will come to realize, with infinite wonder, that the global vision of reality becomes always greater. This movement could be compared to the effect of a stone that, as it falls more deeply into the water, inscribes an ever widening series of circles on the water's surface. We could represent this second moment in the following way:

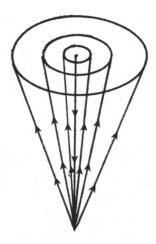

In this way, for example, the person who at a certain point becomes aware of the dynamic nature of the Kingdom of God, which is like a mustard seed, will gradually come to see this dynamism filling the universe and empowering man and his history.

The Religious Character of Signs

From what we have tried to say, the religious character of the method of signs is evident: It is a method conscious of its limits and as such it is filled with veneration for the mystery, which it knows to be unfathomable; it is a method that does not claim to explain, circumscribe, or define, but rather one that speaks falteringly, through hints. The method of signs knows that human language is always an approximation. At the same time, it is a method full of respect for the person and his capacities: in contradistinction to the definition, which must be received by everyone in the same way and at the same time, the sign, which creates space for the individual's personal work of absorption, will be penetrated by each person in a different way—obviously within the limits given by the sign itself—and at a different rhythm.

The method of signs is very helpful for the catechist. When it is correctly used it is impossible to overcontrol the child. In order to exercise control there must be a common measure, and this cannot exist when we use signs, when we try to help the child to enter into the mystery. The catechist who uses the method of signs will find himself in a position of extreme poverty in comparison with the person who holds the apparently secure tools of control; but his poverty is the richness of faith.

Therefore the method of signs educates the child and the catechist in humility (that virtue which has been defined as the "cardinal virtue of the Christian"), because this method never gives anyone the sense of knowing everything, of having arrived at the core of things; given their allusive nature, signs will never be exhausted of their meaning. The goal will always appear beyond us, the horizon will open itself before us as ever expanding. Face to face with the unfathomability of the Christian message and its inexhaustible richness, the person will feel small and great: small in front of the infinite Mystery; great, because it has been given to him to enter it in some way, great with a greatness that is gift.

A group of three- to five-year-old children was praying after the presentation of the baptismal sign of light; the catechist tried to begin the prayer by saying: "What can we say to God, who has given us such a beautiful light as this?" A little girl responded: "That we are small"; a little boy replied: "That we are good"; and immediately another child corrected him: "That He is good"; and the same girl who started the prayer said: "That we are great." Humility and wonder are two interrelated attitudes. In fact the signs, whose meaning will never be depleted, are instruments, without substitute, to keep alive that emotion which we have said is proper to the child and has such importance in the *homo religiosus*.

In the context of the religious value of signs, we would also like to mention that in using such a method it seems to us that one witnesses the collapse of the assertions some people make concerning the impossibility of speaking about Christ to those who have no idea of God. We cannot reach toward the transcendent without taking signs into consideration, and the greatest sign of the Father is Christ, Immanuel (God with us). Signs in some way continue the Incarnation, and every sign derives from Christ, primordial sign, and takes its meaning from Him. Yet the sign, by its very nature, prevents us from limiting ourselves to the sensible world; the sign opens us to the transcendent. The sign becomes therefore an instrument in the education of faith, meaning by faith a way of knowing that goes beyond the sensible. Through signs we become accustomed not to stop at what our eyes see and our hands touch; we become accustomed to search the horizon for a different reality. The initiation into the language of signs bestows a kind of interior agility on the person. Thus, in our estimation, there is not an initial phase of catechesis that is vaguely theistic, one not concretized in the sign, and only secondarily a later phase that is purely Christian. The encounter with Christ, primordial sign, opens to man the infinite space of the transcendent.

NOTES

1. P. Duploye, *La religion de Péguy* (Paris: 1965), p. XI.

2. Alonso-Schoekel, *Il dinamismo della tradizione* (Brescia: Paideia, 1970), pp. 265ff.

3. PL 76, 135.

4. Matthieu (*Vérité et Vie,* [1969–1970], pp. 9–10) warns against the danger of "blocking the biblical message with our own dull guidelines acquired once and for all."

5. S. Marsili, "I sacri segni: storia e presenza. Terminologia segnale nella liturgia," *Liturgia-Nuova Serie* 9 (Padova: 1970), pp. 7–40. Sofia Cavalletti, "Segno, simbolo, tipo nell'ebraismo e nel cristianesimo primitivo," *ibid.,* pp. 41–62.

6. "The Incarnation is the act through which God is "symbolized," that is to say, "signified," see R. Mehl, "Théologie et symbole," *Revue des Sciences Religieuses* (1975), p. 4.

7. D. Otto Via Jr., *The Parables: Their Literary and Existential Dimension* (Philadelphia: Fortress Press, 1967), pp. 70–108.

8. J. Jeremias, *The Parables of Jesus* (New York: Charles Scribner's Sons, 1962). Italian Edition, *Le parabole* (Brescia: Paideia, 1973).

9. A. Alonso-Schoekel, in AA.VV., *La Bibbia nella Chiesa dopo la Dei Verbum* (Roma: Paoline, 1969), pp. 118ff.

10. E. Schillebeeckx, "Culto profano e celebrazione eucaristica," *Rivista di Pastorale Liturgica* (1969), p. 231.

11. E. Sapir, *Language, An Introduction to the Study of Speech* (New York: 1921). Italian Edition *Il linguaggio* (Torino: Einaudi, 1969), p. 4.

12. E. Benveniste, "Nature du signe linguistique" *Linguistica I* (1939), p. 46; same author, *Problèmes de linguistique générale* (Paris, 1960), pp. 26ff.

13. P. Ricoeur, "Parole et symbole," *Revue des Sciences Religieuses* (1975), p. 147.

Chapter Eleven
Anthropological Catechesis

"All are yours; and you are Christ's; and Christ is God's."

1 Corinthians 3:23

On the basis of an interpretation of catechesis that is defined as anthropological because of the attention it gives to man, the departure point for catechetical work ought to be looked for in the person's everyday experience, and going from this to God. Accordingly, catechesis that is not based on experience would be considered abstract and "disincarnate." This is an approach that has become widespread in the last few years, and represents the most current reaction to the intellectualistic and abstract catechetical formulation that preceded it.[1] The religious crisis we are presently living is certainly a crisis of "Incarnation"; for the most part it is not God Who is denied, but Christ Who is rejected; there is a rather diffuse acceptance of the existence of a vague divine person but we do not accept God-made-man, with all the consequences of such an event, and particularly the fact that the Incarnation continues in a special manner in the Liturgy. With the Incarnation under attack, Christians have been led to recognize how little their Christianity was incarnated, how far away it was from real life. The fault for this naturally fell on catechesis as well: Catechesis supplied a quantity of notions, yet it did not inflame life; it was a teaching imparted by a master (in the pejorative sense of the word), not an initiation into the reality lived by a community; it was not rooted in life.

At the Medellin Conference, which marked an important stage in the history of catechesis, it was affirmed that by rediscovering the doctrinal, biblical, and liturgical sources, one half of the path had been walked; the other half remained: renewal by means of a new reference to man.[2] And so today we insist a great deal, and rightly so, on "fidelity to God and to man."[3] According to the present interpretation, the references to man should be looked for in the experiences of everyday life. It is more or less within these experiences that one ought to look for the vital link in catechesis.

Nevertheless this does not seem to us to be the only interpretation of what was stated authoritatively at Medellin. First of all we ask ourselves: Catechesis, the meeting with God's Word, meditation, prayer, are these not of sufficient weight to constitute an experience in themselves? In order to become vital, is it essential that they receive sustenance from experiences that are not directly religious in character? Those children who are captivated by and absorbed in what they have listened to and lived in catechesis, who refer to it by expressing it in words as well in their peaceful and serene state of soul, have these children had an experience of life or not? Is the religious experience necessarily secondary to the nonreligious experience? Why then does even an abandoned child, who has never experienced parental affection, when meeting the Good Shepherd, draw in the center of the page a "happy heart," her own?

But we have even greater doubts regarding anthropological catechesis, understood in the sense of catechesis linked to—and therefore in some manner dependent on—everyday experience. We ask ourselves, in fact, if it is not the fundamental structure of the child that should be taken as the basis and reference point for that necessary "attention to man."

We believe that this indispensable attention is also present when it is the fundamental structure of each age, as we have called it, that is taken into consideration, more than the child's single experiences. The child's psychological configuration is rooted at a deeper level than whatever the child may have lived, in the sense that there are vital *exigencies* that remain alive when they are gratified, but that are also present—almost like an unappeased hunger—even when they do not find their satisfaction.

"Sensitive Periods" and "Constants"

To be clearer maybe it is preferable to offer a short history as to how we reached this conviction. At a certain point in our work we realized that there were some subjects to which children of the same age yet from very different backgrounds always reacted in the same manner. As our experience gradually widened, through collaborators and past students, this fact became always more obvious; the phenomenon was verified in children of middle-class, farming, and factory-worker families; also in gypsy children, and city, suburban, and country children; in Italy, Africa, North and South America. It was evident that there were certain "constants" in children. The children's reactions we have been able to observe can be synthesized in three points:

1. A great desire to continue to listen to specific themes and to continue their personal work with them on their own.
2. A profound sense of serene peace, of enchantment.
3. Some themes become part of the children themselves, as if they had always known them; it is not knowledge that is academic in character, one that comes from the intellectual effort of learning; rather it appears as the result of a vital act, through which the child seems to have received something that corresponds to him in a profound way, and of which the child has need in order to build himself in harmony.

These three points recalled to us what Maria Montessori termed the "sensitive periods"; that is, periods when the child feels himself irresistibly attracted toward specific objects, or, better, toward specific acquisitions, such as language, for example. Nowadays psychologists speak instead of "critical points" in the "programming" of the child's life. In any event, we are dealing with a force that presides over the child's development, a force that requires satisfaction and has, one could say, a fixed schedule. It is the force of life that is being realized through successive stages and tyrannically demands to be actualized.

The characteristics of these "sensitive periods" are a deep interest in an object (for instance, the sounds for language), the presence of a vital impetus that relentlessly tends toward a determinate acquisition; and a sense of enjoyment that involves the whole child and puts him at peace when this need is satisfied (on the contrary, when it is obstructed it provokes violent reactions). The gratification of such an exigence leads to the harmonious construction of the person in himself, and in his relationship to the world; the absence of such satisfaction leads to the extinction of this vital force and to deviations that can negatively affect the child's entire life.

The objects to which the children have always responded in the same manner are:

1. The Good Shepherd parable, received by the younger children primarily as the expression of God's protective love. As we have said this aspect is gradually integrated with other aspects as the child passes from childhood, through adolescence, to the age of maturity.
2. The Paschal mystery presented through the darkness-light contrast, and thus Baptism as the means by which this light of the resurrection is transmitted to mankind, that is, as the participation in the light-life of the risen Christ.
3. The Eucharist as linked to the Good Shepherd parable, and presented as the "sacrament of the gift" of His presence in our life.
4. The parables of the kingdom that present it as a mysterious and powerful reality that is realized in the passage from the small to the great.

In chapter 3 the two cycles of the curriculum were introduced and a diagram was presented to illustrate them. Here we mention only two fundamental themes of the second cycle: a new aspect of the mystery of Christ and His relationship with us as revealed in the parable of the True Vine (John 15:1–10); the liturgical dimension of this parable, that is, the breaking of the bread gesture during the Mass; some moral maxims from the Gospel. These themes correspond to the new needs of the older child: the interest in morality and the beginning of the child's openness to social awareness.

We have observed that each of these foundational points, to which the children have shown themselves especially responsive, is gratifying and reassuring in nature even considered on its own. These themes speak essentially of love given and received (the Good Shepherd knows His sheep by name, He guides, defends, and nourishes them, He gives them His life; the sheep listen to His voice, they gather around Him; He offers His light-life; men accept it and become light-life in their turn). It seems to us that all these points are especially responsive to that religiousness proper to early childhood, which has been defined as feminine or maternal. They respond to the fundamental need that exists in every human being, but that in the child becomes constitutive of his very person: the security of being loved and of having someone to love. This need endures in the child even in the absence of an actual experience of love in his life; it lasts precisely as an *exigence*, which, insofar as it has not been gratified, may become even more profound and more deeply felt. Numerous catechists have noted in those children who are abandoned or in any case little loved a particular "avidity" when faced with the Good Shepherd parable. Therefore, a negative human situation is not adequate reason to resign ourselves to a failure in the realm of catechesis, but rather it becomes an exceedingly valid motive for trying to make catechesis a living encounter of love with God, through His Christ. This does not mean reducing the religious fact to a substitute for what life sometimes does not give; instead, it means that the religious reality responds to what our human nature indispensably needs.

We think that, through the elements indicated above, some foundational needs of the child have been satisfied, some fundamental needs of early childhood have been nourished with religious good. Consequently, we can say that our catechesis is anthropological, in that it takes into consideration not the single experiences of the individual child, but the general structure and needs of the child himself.

Experience and Exigence

The difference between experience (*esperienza*) and exigence (*esigenza*) is very great. To link catechesis to an experience means to touch things that have already been lived, for good or ill, and that therefore will inevitably condition what we try to base on it; it means to find a field already tilled and at times ruined by life. To seek to satisfy an exigence is instead to slake a thirst, to nourish a potentiality. When we try to base catechesis on a child's experience, sometimes we find ourselves before a flower that has already faded; if we try to make catechesis satisfy the child's exigencies, we will find ourselves as if faced with a mouth opened wide in eagerness. We believe we should serve life at the profound level of exigence.

We ask ourselves if the secret of that avidity we have noted so many times in the child, of that readiness with which he takes possession of certain elements of the Christian message, and also of that joy which the child has let us witness in his meeting with God does not reside in the fact that our catechesis is of this second type. Nothing is more gratifying than the satisfaction of a vital exigence. Therefore, we think the situation to be thus: Certain exigencies exist in the innermost depths of the child; if the Christian message is presented in such a way as to satisfy these, the child will appropriate the message with a vital impulse, and will then be capable of reliving it in his everyday experience.

Many examples reported in this book—especially those relating to the Good Shepherd, whose resemblance the children refind in the person they love most—and the resonance that specific themes have on the older child's behavior after six years of age seem to us proof that the message does remain open to the child's individual experiences, that it has been received in a personal way, and, therefore, that it is essentially rooted in the child's life. When the child's fundamental exigence is satisfied, this is reflected in his relationships and in his way of acting. The child unites together the message and life in a simple and spontaneous connection.

A mode of presentation that precludes the catechist from making direct links seems to allow room for a greater range of application, because any specific reference is limiting. Furthermore, it seems to us more respectful of the child to avoid touching in direct form those affective chords that should not be touched, or of which the child has every right to be jealous.

The Aspect of God the Child Seeks

For catechesis to be a living event for the child, the catechist should know the child's *exigencies* and *the aspect of God* that most corresponds to them. It is a commonly held opinion that magic plays a great role in the religiousness of the child; an opinion like this is based on scientific studies that, however, according to Milanesi's important observations, are "able to evidence the magical features of the religious teaching imparted to the child, but [they are] not conclusive in demonstrating if, or how much, the psychical structure of the subject is predisposed to accept a magical stimulus."[4] Milanesi also states: "More than a negation of reality, magical activity expresses the need for a different world."[5] If we accept this explanation of magic, then we ask ourselves: Why should the child have the need to shape a "different" religious world? Is God unable to satisfy the child's aspirations? Or is it perhaps that the adult has not managed to present, from among the many aspects of God, the one that corresponds to the exigencies of the child's age? "God is love" says Saint John; but love has many faces: What is the face of God the child needs?

The image of God as bridegroom appears frequently in the Bible; it is the aspect of God that responds to the needs of adolescents after fifteen years of age, but it would say nothing to the young child. It is significant that in the catechetical experience we have tried to describe—in which the Good Shepherd's protective love is central—we have not noted any traces of magic in the children. At any rate, accepting Milanesi's point of view, we believe it is urgent that catechists search for the face of God the children need.

R. Vianello observes that the child's psychic structure blocks the assimilation of certain religious conceptions such as God as all-powerful and omnipresent, God as Spirit.[6] If God were exhausted in these aspects, we would have to give up speaking to the children about Him. But we believe that God is not so poor as that. What is poor is our research of the way in which to present God to the child.

It is obvious that a catechesis founded on the child's exigencies follows a method that is perhaps more indirect than the one based on the child's experiences. Nonetheless, we wonder if in the realm of the Spirit it is ever possible to give a direct aid. We seek, as we have said, to nourish a certain "hunger" in the child with religious food; then it will be up to the child to sustain his daily life with this food. In some manner we provide the instruments that the child must use by himself; we follow a method that responds to the child's unspoken request: "Help me to do it by myself."

NOTES

1. L. Erdozain, "L'évolution de la catéchèse," *Lumen Vitae* (1969), pp. 575–599.

2. Cf. Medellin Documents, *Liberation*: Towards a Theology for the Church in the World, According to the Second General Conference of Latin American Bishops, Medellin, 1968 (Rome: Catholic Book Agency, 1972). Italian Edition, *Medellin-Documenti* (Bologna: Dehoniane, 1969).

3. *Il Rinnovamento della catechesi,* no. 160; see R. Gianna-telli, "Linee di metodologia catechistica," *Il Rinnovamento della catechesi in Italia* (Roma: Università Salesiana, 1970), pp. 105–121.

4. G. Milanesi, *Psicologia della religione* (Torino-Leumann: LDC, 1974), pp. 147ff.

5. *Ibid.,* p. 150.

6. R. Vianello, *op. cit.,* p. 265.

Conclusion

Reaching the end of our brief exposition, we would like to re-emphasize a phenomenon that has become clear to us through observation: the convergence of the various elements presented to the children and their fusion into a synthesis, evident in the children's discussions and many of their works, in which the figure of the Good Shepherd is often the catalyst. Such syntheses, as we have mentioned elsewhere, were born in the children's minds even before the catechists themselves were aware of them. This fact led us to ask ourselves the question: What is the profound relationship that binds together the subjects listed in the preceding chapter? We seem able to synthesize this connection as the passage from a less to a more: The Good Shepherd gives His life, but for the purpose that men may also have it and "have it abundantly" (John 10:10); the paschal mystery, presented through the images of darkness and light, is the passage from a negative to a positive; it is the diffusion of light that has conquered the darkness. In the parables of the kingdom we have mentioned, the passage from the less to the more is visualized in the transformation of the small seed into the great tree and the full ear of wheat, of the lump of dough into the leavened loaf of bread.

This, it seems to us, is the fundamental law of life, as incredible as it may seem: Life develops through a series of successive "deaths," which lead us to live always more fully, because in each death there is the seed of the resurrection. The secret of reality seems to be that it always preserves in itself the seed of the resurrection, and the more the seed is reduced and hidden, the more powerful it becomes. What we call death is the diminishing of the force of life to its most imperceptible expression; but it is from the most tenuous forms of life that—paradoxically—life blossoms ever richer. We see this being realized in nature: "Un-

176

less a grain of wheat falls into the earth and dies, it remains alone; but if it dies, it bears much fruit" (John 12:24); yet Jesus said this alluding to Himself. This is a law we see being realized in man as well, both on the physical and psychical planes. The Bible constantly proposes this fact to us: Fundamental in the Old Testament is the doctrine of the "remnant" of Israel, that is, that little group which is open to God's Word and its demands, through which the thread of this people's history remains alive and slowly ascends toward greater realizations. The New Testament suggests the same fact to us in parabolic form and in the explicit enunciation of Paul: "Power is made perfect in weakness," "for when I am weak, then I am strong" (2 Corinthians 12:9–10). And, finally, this universal law is assumed and lived by Christ, consciously and freely, as an act of love for the Father and for mankind; it resulted in a new richness of life, which He communicates to all creatures. If we were capable of seeing the Christian proclamation with that essentiality of which the child is master we would see in it the concretization of a universal process, on the level of full and conscious love and on the level of history; we would see in it the realization of what is most simple, and therefore most essential in the created world.

At this point we would like to return for a moment to the question we posed at the beginning of this book: Is it justifiable to give the child a religious formation? Now we seem able to give a more complete response. From the psychological point of view, it appeared to us that the child finds in the religious experience, and in the Christian message in particular, the satisfaction of deep, vital exigencies necessary to the harmonious construction of his person. As to the content, the proclamation of the death and resurrection—the synthesis of the Christian kerygma—is the revelation of the fundamental law of life; it is the initiation into the knowledge of the reality in which we live.

Therefore, far from building superstructures, to initiate the child into the Christian mystery is to initiate the child into the mystery of life. To bar the child from the religious experience, to preclude the possibility of his receiving the Christian message, is to betray the child's most profound exigencies, to block his access to the full knowledge of the reality in which he finds himself immersed.

It is not insignificant that Maria Montessori—whose capacity to see children cannot be denied, whether one is a Montessorian or not—observed (during the time of her first experiment in this field in Barcelona, in 1915) that the children not only showed a "pleasing sense of joy" in contact with the religious reality, but a "new dignity" as well.[1] The child—the child of whom it is said that "there is no being more metaphysical"—has shown joy and a particular dignity when the doors of the infinite are opened to him.

Today we try to be so attentive to, so respectful of, the child's needs; how serious it would be then to stop at the threshold of the child's deepest exigence: the opening to the transcendent. There is the risk of awakening needs in the child without then giving him *all* the means necessary to satisfy them. There is the risk of letting the child take a leap forward with a thrust that would fall back on him due to the lack of a worthy object—like a missile launched toward marvelous objectives that, at a certain point, loses its momentum and falls; like a flower at the point of full bloom that, at a certain moment, bows its head and withers. The "metaphysical" child, the "essential" child, will find the full realization of himself only in the world of the transcendent, a world in which he has shown he moves completely at his ease.

NOTES

1. Maria Montessori, *The Child in the Church,* p. 24. Italian Edition, *I bambini viventi nella Chiesa,* p. 15.

Appendix

Explanations of the Drawings

Fig. 1. Quite often two houses appear in the children's drawings. Virginia (five years old) explained: "My house and the house of Jesus" (Casa dei Bambini Montessori, Viale Spartaco 12, Rome). It is known that in children's drawings, the house indicates the mother and expresses protection.

Fig. 2. Giovanna (four years old) has never gone to church, but she too represents her house (with a light) and God's house (with two lights) (Casa dei Bambini "Adele Costa Gnocchi," Rome).

Fig. 3. Here the "house of Jesus" takes the color of light (five years old, Viale Spartaco, Rome).

Fig. 4. For Alessia (four years old), the paschal candle is much higher than her house (Casa dei Bambini "Adele Costa Gnocchi").

Fig. 5. The boy (five years old) explained that he put two children among the sheep because "while he was working" he understood that we are the sheep (Suore del Salvatore, Monteverde, Rome).

Fig. 6. The Good Shepherd calls His sheep by name. The figure on the right represents the Madonna (six years old).

Fig. 7. Giovanna (five years old) has drawn a sheepfold and a house, symbol of the mother, and therefore of protection and security (Via degli Orsini, Rome).

179

Fig. 8. [Fig. 23]   Two examples of the way the work develops with the older children. Simone (ten years old) has synthesized the two moments of the epiclesis and the offering (Via degli Orsini, Rome). Barbara (eleven years old) has also synthesized the moment of the epiclesis (the dove and light) and the offering, trying to specify what our response consists of: The sheep represents a person, the commandments, the Gospel maxims, and the example of the drawing at the right indicates our moral obligation. The writing on the right stresses the importance of man's work (Via degli Orsini, Rome).

Fig. 9.   At the top of the page there are sheep without light, and luminous sheep (note the yellow-orange colored heart) together with persons who hold a lighted candle. At the center, there is the heart, in which it is written "*qore* felice" "happy hart" (the original is misspelled). Farther down the page there is an altar and beside it the words "Little girls have light" and beneath it: "I love you so much Mommy." The church at the bottom is called "the house of light"; sheep are going toward it carrying lighted candles. The catechist watched the little girl draw a house first and then she changed it into a church. When the work was finished, the catechist asked her the reason for this and she replied: "Because the sheep's house is the church" (five years old; Suore dell'Amore Misericordioso, Borgata Casilina, Rome).

Fig. 10.   Note the semicircle, the sign of protection and sense of security, and the flowers, which take the place of the Shepherd's hands (five years old).

Fig. 11.   Note the color yellow, expression of joy. Some sheep are without a name: "Not because they don't have one, but because I got tired," said the child who drew the picture (five years old; Borgata Casilina, Rome).

Fig. 12.   Note the disproportion between the dimensions of the Shepherd and the wolf (five and a half years old; Borgata Casilina, Rome).

Fig. 13.   The austerity of the three crosses contrasts with the colors of the two figures drawn between the crosses and the flowers. The little girl wrote: "Jesus, you gave us life. The Good Shepherd ... Jesus you are risen. Jesus I love you. Jesus ..." (six years old; Borgata Casilina, Rome).

Fig. 14. In the center there is the figure of the Good Shepherd and the sheep; at the bottom right is a cross; at the left is the paschal candle, a heart, and a little candle: "The heart has the light and the candle is lit" (six years old, Borgata Casilina, Rome).

Fig. 15. The little boy explained to the catechist: "The lamb is really happy." "Why?" asked the catechist. The boy replied: "Because it is with God." Beside the lamb is the baptismal sign of light (six years old; Nostra Signora di Lourdes, Rome).

Fig. 16. Anna Laura (six years old) drew an altar in the center of the page with a lighted candle underneath; the sheepfold on the right is matched by the church on the left (six years old; Borgata Casilina, Rome).

Fig. 17. An interesting synthesis drawn by a four-year-old boy: the Good Shepherd, the epiclesis, and communion of the Mass (Nostra Signora di Lourdes, Rome).

Fig. 18. The sheepfold of the Good Shepherd and the Eucharistic table are drawn one on top of the other (six years old, Borgata San Basilio, Rome).

Fig. 19. Maurizio (six years old) unites sheep and people together around the altar (Suore Sacramentine, Borgata San Basilio, Rome).

Fig. 20. The Good Shepherd, altar, sheep, and a person are enclosed together in a circle, which is reminiscent of the sheepfold (Suore Sacramentine, Borgata San Basilio, Rome).

Fig. 21. The unity between Christ and His faithful at Mass is emphasized by the round form given to the altar, which recalls the sheepfold (five years old, Monteverde, Rome).

Fig. 22. For Stefania (five years old) the synthesis between the Good Shepherd parable and the Mass is so complete that she draws the altar in the form of a meadow (Monteverde, Rome).

Fig. 23. See explanation for number 8.

Fig. 24. For Roberta (five years old) the altar is the body of Christ and also of those who share in the Eucharist (Monteverde, Rome).

Fig. 25. A four-and-a-half year old boy, after tracing the image of the Good Shepherd, pasted the paschal candle beside it.

Fig. 26. A cross is drawn beside the Good Shepherd, Who is shining with light; He is seen therefore in a paschal perspective. The lamb is "His lamb of light" (five and a half years old; Via Casilina, Rome).

Fig. 27. The Good Shepherd's light is also the light of the sheep. Note the cross and the paschal candle at the bottom (six years old; Via Casilina, Rome).

Fig. 28. The paschal candle dominates the center of the arch. A sheep, of which only the head is depicted, "is going to get the light of Jesus." Note the difference of proportion between this candle and the child's baptismal candle, at bottom right. Beside the paschal candle is the "Gospel of Jesus." The two containers for the baptismal oils (bottom right) are shining with light, as are the two human figures and all the sheep in the fold (bottom left) (six years old).

Fig. 29. The Good Shepherd's light (paschal candle in center) is "red because be gives His life, yellow, because he is full of light." A sheep is depicted as taking this light (Suore Missionarie Francescane di Maria, Via Appia Nuova 522, Rome).

Fig. 30. The symbols of the baptismal gown and the light surrounding the sheep indicate the connection between the Good Shepherd parable and Baptism (Via degli Orsini, Rome).

Fig. 31. The synthesis of the death, resurrection, and our participation in the light-life of the risen Christ (six years old; Suore Missionarie Francescane di Maria, Via Appia Nuova, Rome).

Fig. 32. Maria Pia (four years old) has placed the Holy Spirit in the center of the sheet, colored in yellow, the color of light. The same color is found in the paschal candle, the candles the children are holding, and in the clothes of the persons themselves (Casa dei Bambini, Via Livenza, Rome).

Fig. 33. The connection between Shepherd and sheep is indicated here by the cross. Each sheep has a name (six years old; Istituto Assunzione, Rome).

Fig. 34. A synthesis of Baptism, Good Shepherd parable, and the Eucharist (six years old; Nostra Signora di Lourdes, Rome).

Fig. 35. A drawing on Baptism. The figure at the left is "the newborn baby who is receiving the light"; the figure on the right is Jesus. The house in the center expresses the sense of security and protection that the proclamation has given the child (Paola, five years old; Via degli Orsini, Rome).

Fig. 36. Note the Holy Spirit drawn above the stable to indicate the marvelous birth (eleven years old; Missione Cattolica, Pala, Ciad).

Fig. 37. The Nativity is linked to Easter, represented by the paschal candle; our participation in this mystery is indicated by the baptismal symbols on the bottom left: the cross, baptismal gown (twelve years old; Missione Cattolica, Pala, Ciad).

Fig. 38. A synthesis of Christmas and Easter: There is a star over an enclosed area that makes one think of the cave, but inside Jesus is depicted on the cross, surrounded by angels. This picture was drawn during the Christmas season (five years old; Monteverde, Rome).

Fig. 39. Another synthesis of Christmas and Easter. On the left-hand side of the page Jesus is drawn as a child, in the center as crucified but living. The yellow color of light predominates, which expresses joy (five years old: Monteverde, Rome).

Fig. 40. The figure of the risen Jesus stands over the crib in the center of the page (five years old; Monteverde, Rome).

Fig. 41. In the lower level of the stable there is the crib, in the upper level are the sheep and the Good Shepherd (six years old; Borgata Casilina, Rome).

Fig. 42. The yellow background is the stable; on the lower level in the center there is the figure of the child Jesus, but the scene is dominated by the Good Shepherd. At right, there is one of the Magi (six years old; Nostra Signora di Lourdes, Rome).

Fig. 43. Jesus is illustrated on the cross, to the right of the page; whereas the light of the resurrection dominates the scene (five years old; Nostra Signora di Lourdes, Rome).

Fig. 44. A synthesis of various elements in a drawing done during the Easter season: The child Jesus is in the center, with a lighted candle on either side, which recalls the altar; there are also two sheep and two persons (five years old; Casa dei Bambini di Via Livenza, Rome).

Fig. 45. The child Jesus, top left, is resplendent with light, which makes one think of the risen Jesus. Beside this figure are drawn the Good Shepherd and the Eucharistic symbols of His presence (drawing done during the Christmas season by Abi, five and a half years old; Monclova, Mexico).

Fig. 46. The connection between the Nativity and the Eucharist: The child Jesus "dreams" of the altar (six years old; Borgata San Basilio, Rome).

Fig. 47. Giulio has linked Christmas with the Last Supper (four years old; Casa dei Bambini "Adele Costa Gnocchi," Rome).

Fig. 48. The parable of the hidden treasure: "The farmer has the treasure in his heart" (six years old; Borgata Casilina, Rome).

Fig. 49. A synthesis of the parable of the pearl, the grain of wheat, and Baptism (six years old; Casa della Bambina, Via Laurentina, Rome).

Fig. 50. Another synthesis of the parable of the pearl and Baptism (six years old; Via Laurentina, Rome).

Translation of Drawing Captions

Fig. 8.   "Explanation. This drawing represents the Eucharist
               The hands turned down are the symbol of the gift

The hands turned up are the symbol of the gift
and the vine the chalice and the host (are)
Jesus
and the fruits (are) our good actions"

Fig. 9. "sheep Jesus light" (top of page)
"happy heart"
"all the little girls have light" (words above altar)
"I love you so much Mommy" (words beneath altar)
"house of light" (bottom left hand)

Fig. 12. "Jesus I love you very very much
Jesus I want to stay always close to you
give us lots of light
we are these sheep"

Fig. 13. "Jesus you gave us life" (top)
"The Good Shepherd" "The two thieves" (crosses)
"Jesus you are risen (words beneath crosses)
Jesus I love you
Jesus dear"

Fig. 14. "The Shepherd gives life to his sheep
and he loves all his sheep very much
and he gives them his life and
he makes them become better" (words at top)
"The heart has the light and the candle is lit" (bottom left)
"The Good Shepherd is Jesus" (bottom right)

Fig. 16. "Jesus takes the little girl for a walk" (left of altar)
"The Madonna and Jesus" (right of altar)

Fig. 17. "Our body is the temple of the Holy Spirit" (words between hands)
The Ten Commandments
I am the Lord your God
1 you shall have no other gods before me
2 you shall not take the name of
the Lord your God in vain
3 observe the sabbath day to keep it holy
4 honor your father and your mother that your days
may be prolonged in the land

    5 you shall not kill

    6 you shall not bear false witness against your neigh-
bor

    7 you shall not commit adultery

    8 you shall not steal

    9 you shall not covet your neighbor's wife and you
shall not desire your neighbor's house, his field, or
his maidservant, or his ass, or anything that is your
neighbor's

   10 you shall not desire anything that is your neighbor's

"My workbook, that is my work" (top left)

"Be perfect just as your heavenly Father is perfect"
(bottom left)

"When you give alms sound no trumpet before you"

"Love your enemies"

"The grapes God gives us we transform into wine
with our work" (top right)

"Example 'I am cold, I am hungry'" (drawing at
right in box)

"I give you bread, take it"

Fig. 26.   "Jesus and the lost sheep and Jesus is close to his lamb
of light and the lamb always stays close to the light and
does not go far from the Good Shepherd"

Fig. 27.   "Jesus I am sorry that the sheep are separated from
you they do not love you anymore I always want to be
near you and I will never go away from [being] close to
you and I want the light in my heart always"

Fig. 28.   "The sheep are full of light and goodness" (top left)
"A little lamb is born and it is going to get the light of
Jesus" (top right)

Fig. 29.   "The Good Shepherd is red because he gives his life,
yellow because he is full of light" (top)
"The cross is red because Jesus died for us" (center)
"The oil because it gives strength" (bottom)

Fig. 30.   "The light of Christ and the sheep"

Fig. 31.   "The little boy holds the candle in his hand

He has life like the risen Jesus" (top left)

"The little girl with a candle in her hand" (center)

"The paschal candle is like the risen Jesus" (bottom left)

"This is Jesus on the cross" (bottom right)

"Baptism I received the light of Jesus and the white gown" (top left)

"and I became a sheep of Jesus" (center)

"and I can participate at Mass" (bottom right)

Fig. 46. "Today there is no sun because there is the light of God"

Fig. 48. "The farmer sells all he has and will buy that treasure" (top)

"The farmer has the treasure in his heart" (bottom)

Fig. 49. "The parables of Jesus" (top)

"The precious stone" (bottom left)

"The white gown" (center)

"Cross of salvation" (bottom right)

"The grain of wheat (that has) grown" (center right)

Fig. 50. "The gift of baptism" (top)

"The little white gown" (center)

"The lighted candle" (bottom left)

"The precious stone" (bottom right)

Index of Presentations

To be used with the diagram on page 64.

Fig. 1

Fig. 2

GESU

Fig. 3

Fig. 4

Fig. 5

Fig. 6

Fig. 7

Fig. 8

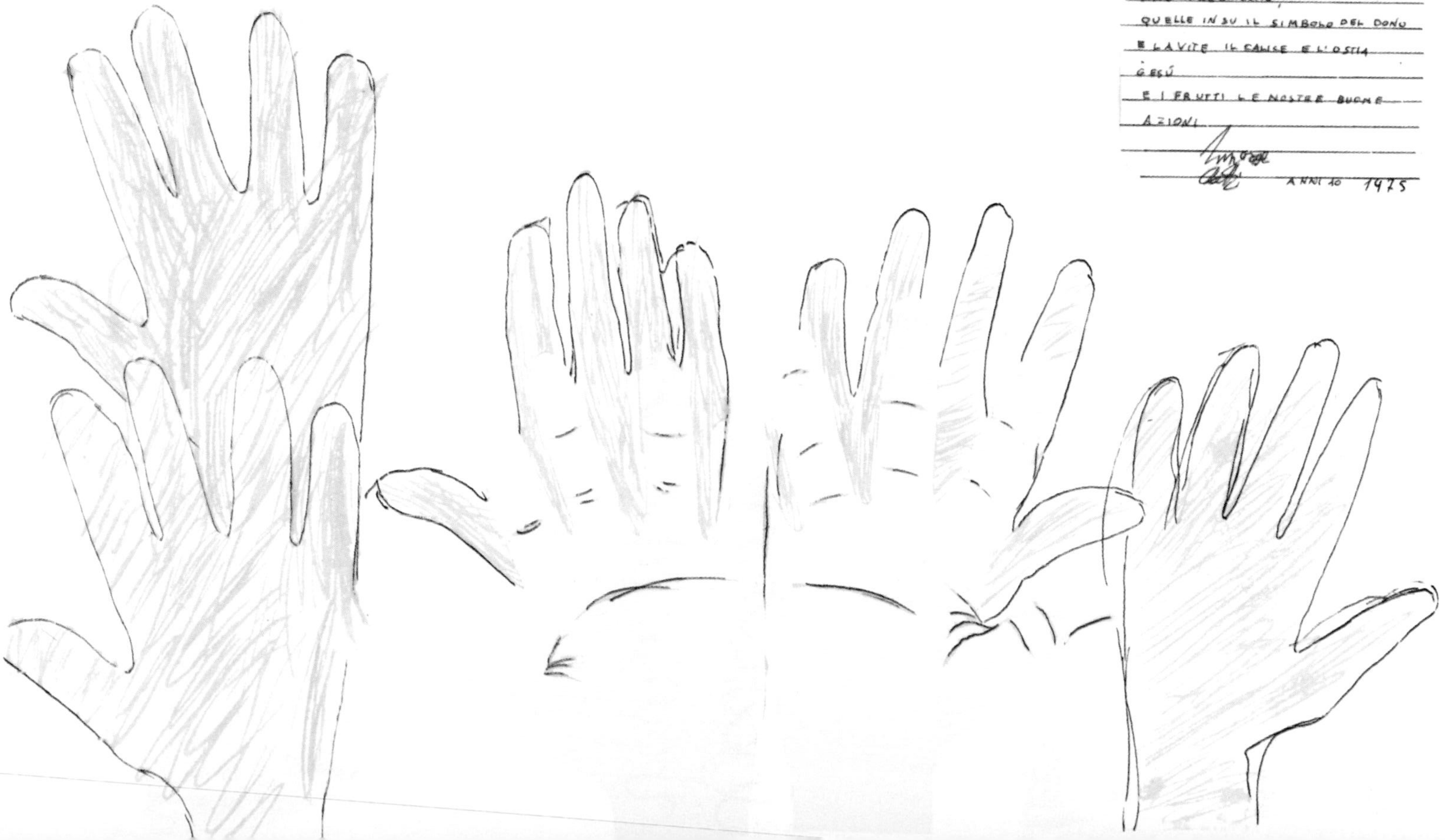

SPIEGAZIONE

QUESTO DISEGNO RAPPRESENTA

L'EUCARESTIA.

LE MANI RIVOLTE IN GIÙ SONO IL

SIMBOLO DEL DONO,

QUELLE IN SU IL SIMBOLO DEL DONO

GESÙ

E LA VITE IL CALICE E L'OSTIA

E I FRUTTI LE NOSTRE BUONE

AZIONI

ANNI 10 1975

pecriele Geoveono

lebabrne
vano apecre i coesdut teb
porte

mamma tivo
gliotouto bane

casa dela luce simona
rali

Fig. 9

DEBORA

Fig. 10

Fig. 11

Gesù ti voglio tantatanto
bene Gesù voglio stare sempre
vicino a te daci tanta luce
queste pecorelle siamo noi

Maria Rita Uttoni

Fig. 12

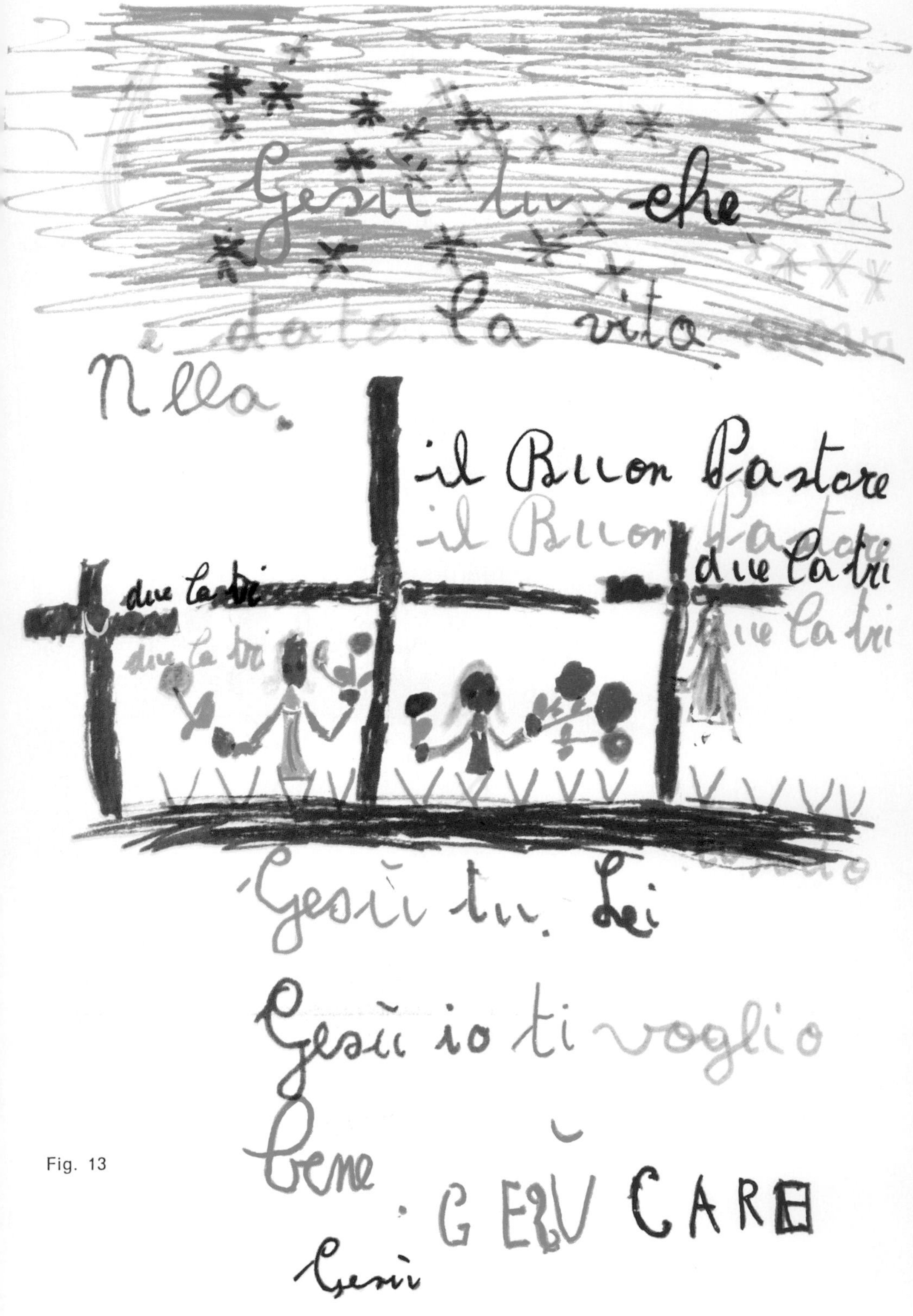
Gesù tu che
dato la vita
Nella
il Buon Pastore
il Buon Pastore
due la tri
due la tri
due la tri
due la tri
Gesù tu Lei
Gesù io ti voglio
bene
GESU CARE
Gesù

Fig. 13

il natura da la vita alle sue pecorelle
e vuole tanto bene a tutte le pecore
ne e gli ola la sua vita e gli
fa di ventare più buona

Sa , Conte mari

Il buon

Il cuore
cia la sua
e se entra a cero

Fig. 14

MATTURINI

Fig. 15

Fig. 16

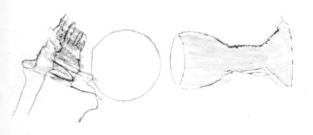

Fig. 17

Fig. 18

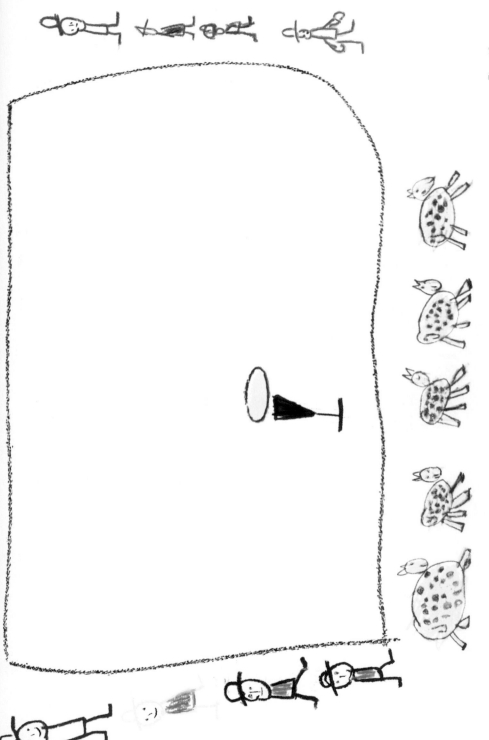

Fig. 19

Fig. 20

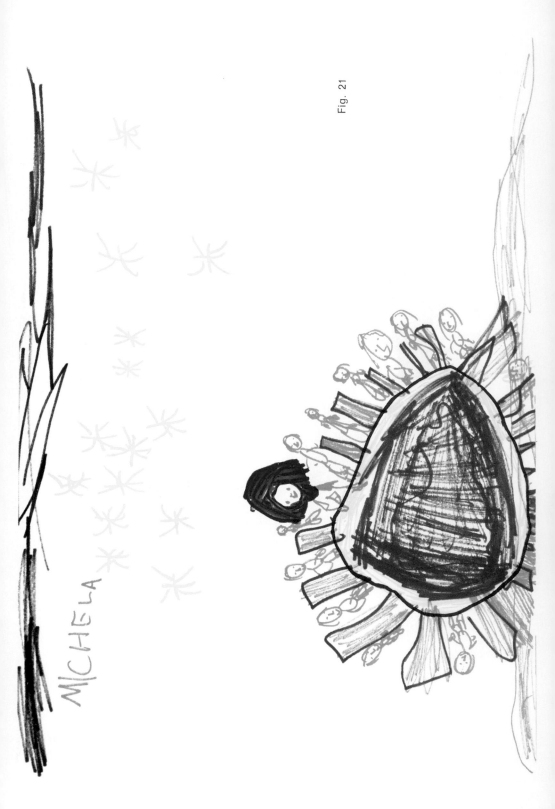

Fig. 21

MICHELA

STEFANÍA

Fig. 22

Il mio quaderno, cioè il mio lavoro

I 10 comandamenti
io sono il Signore Dio tuo

1 non avrai altri dei all'mio cospetto

2 non userai il nome di Dio inutilmente

3 ricordati della festa per santificarla

4 onorerai il padre la madre acciochè tu viva lungamente sopra la terra

5 non uccidere

6 non dirai contro il tuo prossimo testimonianza falsa

7 non commettere atti impuri

8 non rubare

9 non desiderare la donna del tuo compagno ne la casa, ne il tuo asino ne il suo campo ne il suo servo ne il suo bue.

10 non desiderare nulla di quanto appartiene a un altro.

I H S

Siate perfetti come è perfetto il padre vostro

Amate i vostri nemici

Quando fai l'elemosina non suonare le trombe davanti a te.

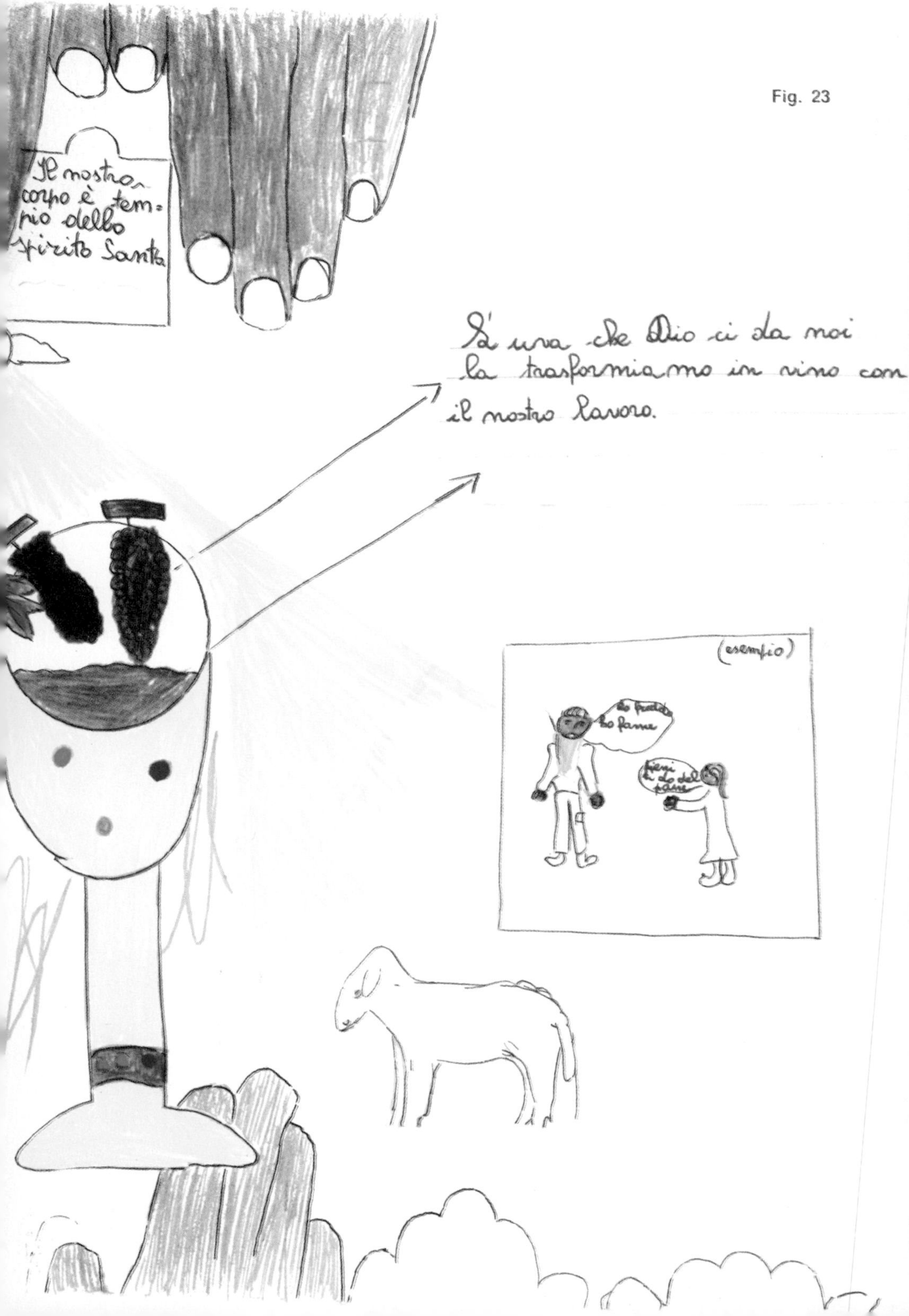
Il nostro corpo è tempio dello spirito Santo
L'uva che Dio ci da noi la trasformiamo in vino con il nostro lavoro.
(esempio)
ho fame
tieni ti do del pane

Fig. 23

ROB
ROBERTA
MEZI

Fig. 24

Il buon Pastore

Fig. 25

Gesù e la pecorella smaritta
e Gesù sta vicino alla sua
pecorella. di luce leista sem=
re vicino al luce e non site
re allontonare dal brion
Pastore.

A voglio
Rita Maria

Fig. 26

Gesù mi di spiace che
ti sono scapate le pecore
non ti vogliono più
bene io voglio stare
sempre vicino a te
e non mi allontano
mia da vicino a te
e voglio sempre
pagni la luce nel
quore

Fig. 27

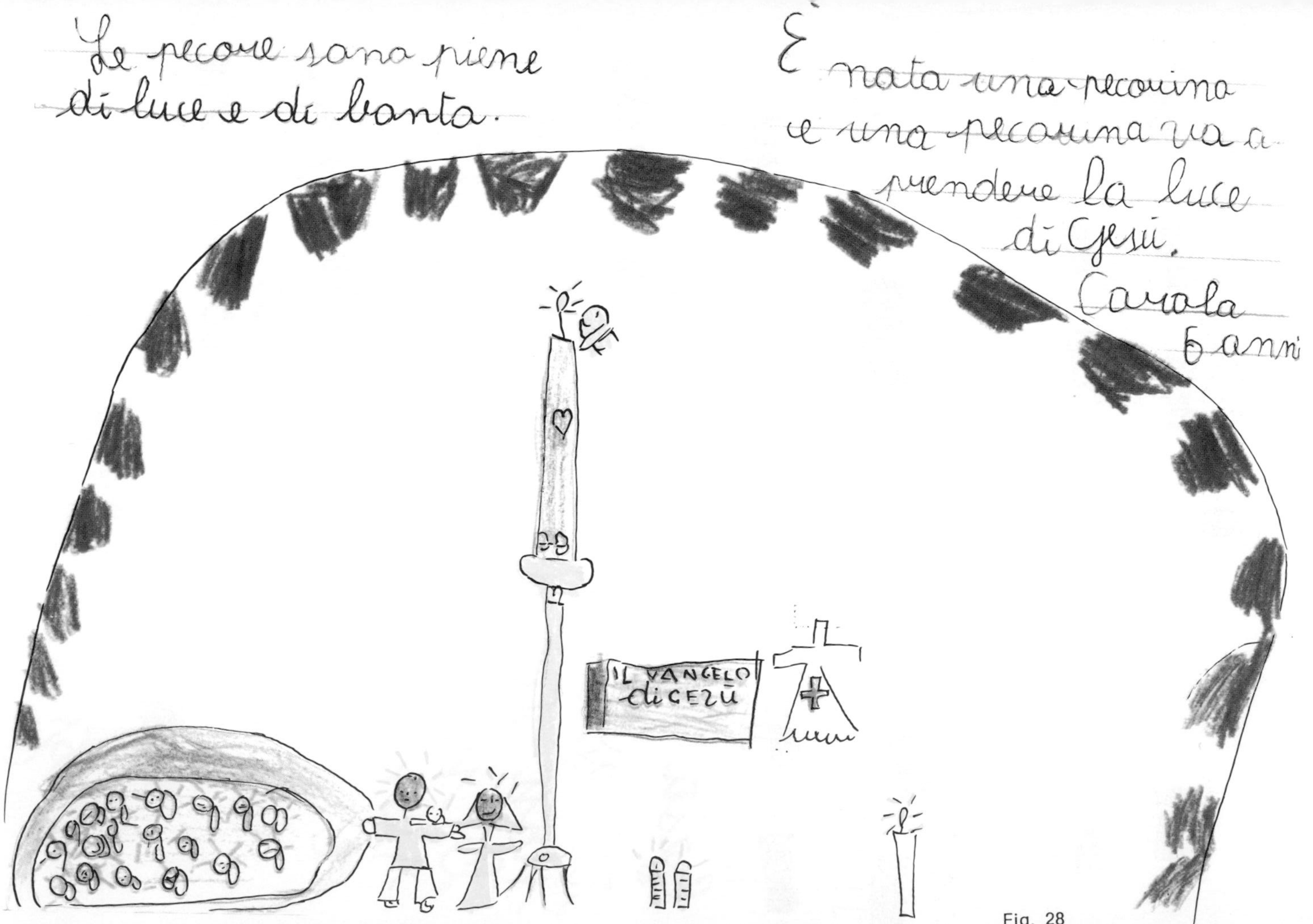
Le pecore sono piene
di luce e di bonta.
È nata una pecorina
e una pecorina va a
prendere la luce
di Gesù.
Carola
6 anni
IL VANGELO
di GEZÙ

Fig. 28

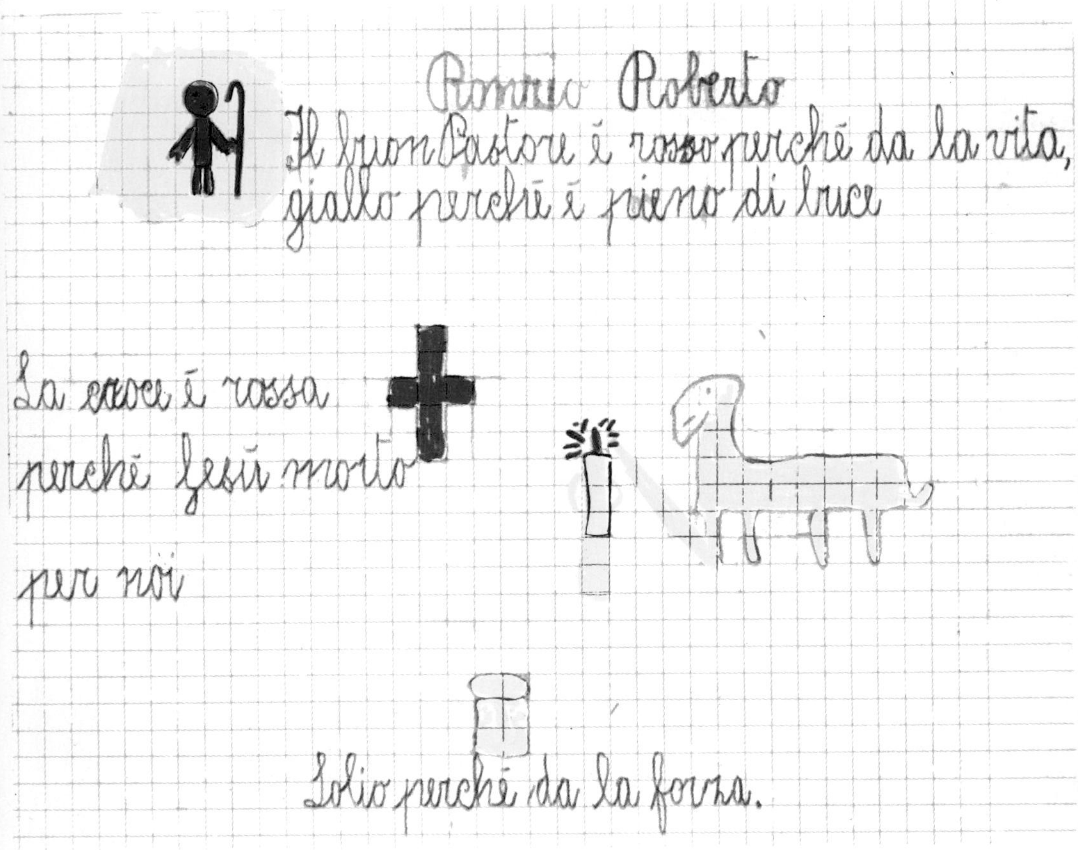

Romeo Roberto

Il buon Pastore è rosso perchè da la vita, giallo perchè è pieno di luce

La croce è rossa perchè Gesù morto per noi

Lolio perchè da la forza.

Fig. 29

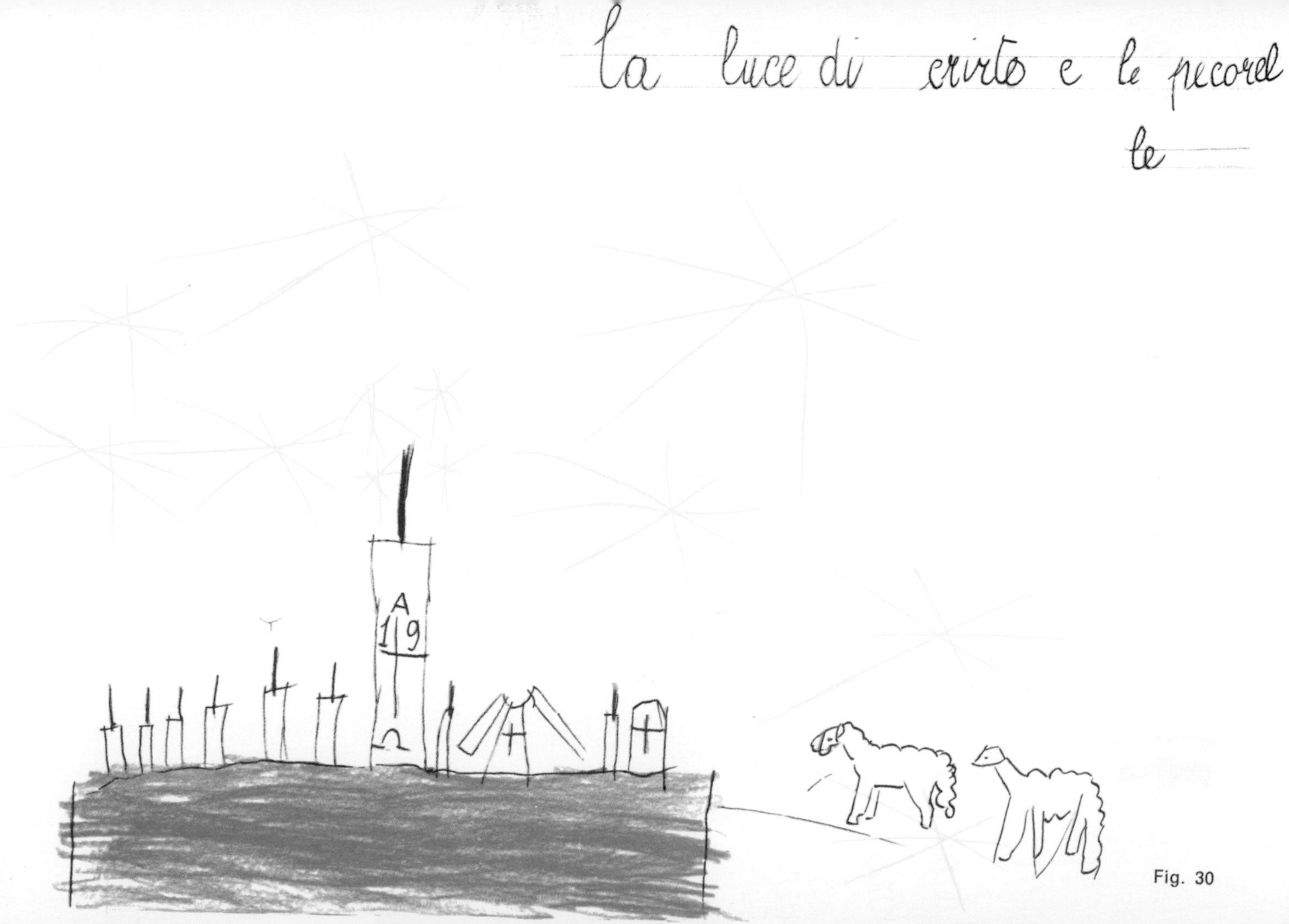

la luce di cristo e le pecore

le ——

Fig. 30

l bambino tiene la.   Roberto Ronnio.

Candela in mano
A la vita come Gesù
Gesù
risolto.

La bambi
na con

la candela in mano.

il cielo: pasquale
e come Gesù risol
to.

Questo e Gesù
in croce.

Fig. 31

Fig. 32

il buon'pastore

marta

Roberta

Lolita madre chiara

yoyi

Fig. 33

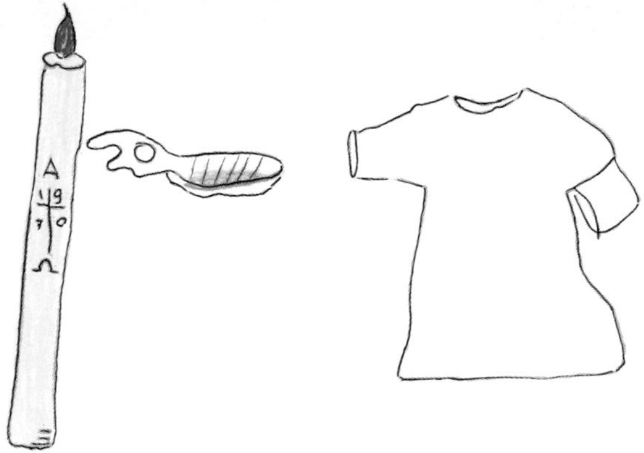

Carlo
anni 6

Fig. 34

al Battesimo io ho ricevuto la luce di Gesù
e la veste candida

e sono diventato una
pecorella di Gesù

e posso partecipare
alla Messa

Fig. 25

Fig. 36

Fig. 37

Fig. 38

Fig. 39

Fig. 40

Fig. 41

Fig. 42

Fig. 43

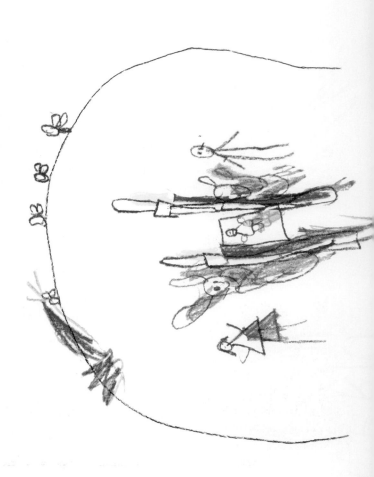

Fig. 44

ABi

Fig. 45

Fig. 46

Fig. 47

il contadino vendette tutto e comperò N 1

quel tesoro.

il contadino ha il tesoro nel cuore

Bruno Latinia

Fig. 48

le parabole di Gesù

il chicco di grano cresciuto

✝ ✝ ✝

✝

croce è della salvezza

..roce è della salvezza

la veste candida

la perla preziosa

Fig. 49

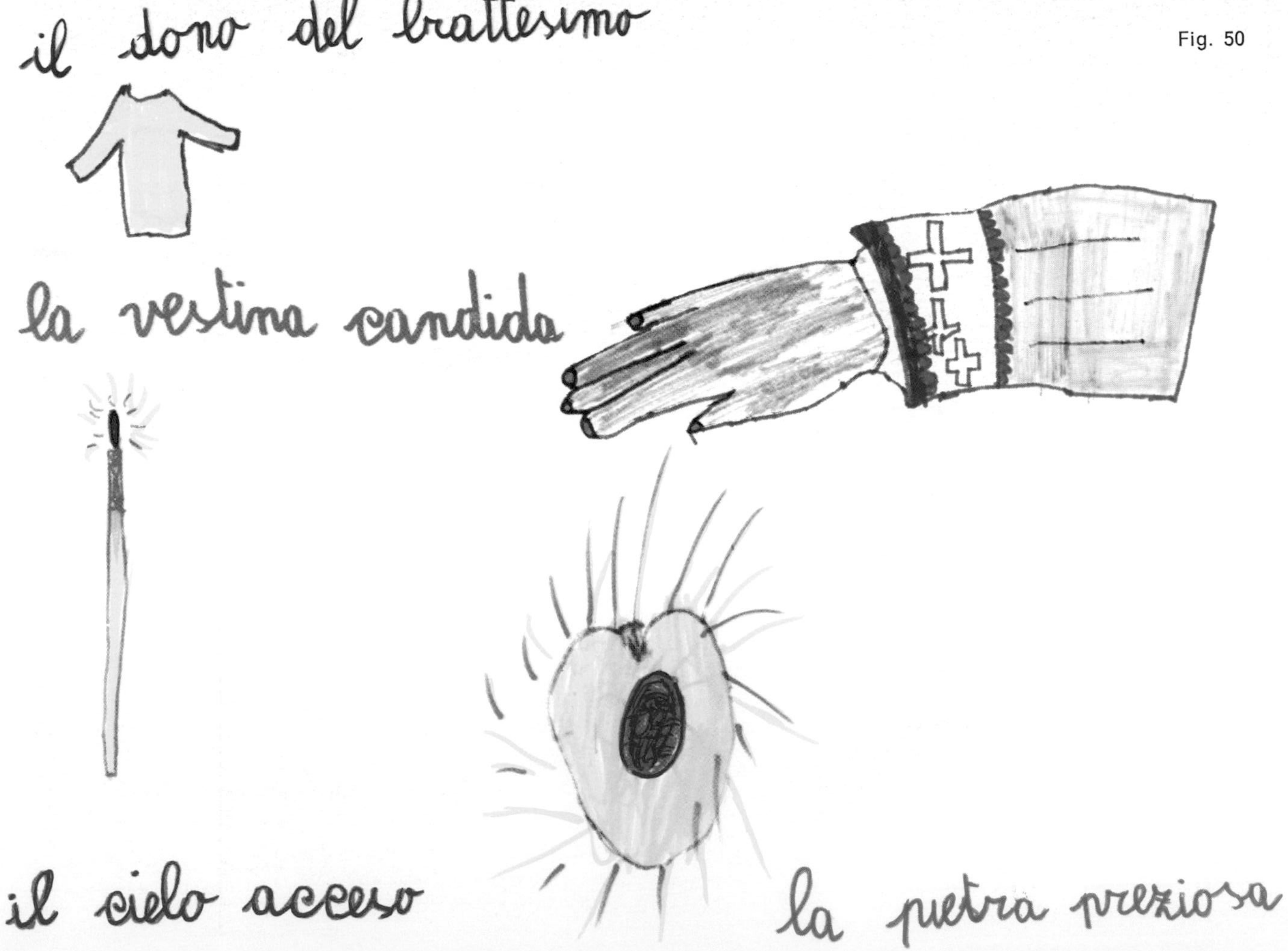

il dono del battesimo

la vestina candida

la pietra preziosa

il cielo acceso

Fig. 50

A child learns how to prepare an altar.

An atrium made in the stable of a convent of the Francescane Missionarie di Maria, Via Appia, Rome.

An "atrium" arranged in the small organ loft in the parish of St. Maria in Aquiro, Rome.

Young children at work in the atrium at Via degli Orsini, Rome.

Three-year-old girl examining the mustard seed at Christian Family Montessori School in Mt. Rainier, Maryland.

Lupita reads the text of the Good Shepherd parable to Kiria. Chicxulub, Mexico.

Individual work with the Good Shepherd material leads to a contemplative inner dialogue. Buenos Aires, Argentina.

Work on the Mass: Christina mixes the few drops of water with the wine in the chalice.

Work on the Mass: the moment of the epiclesis (the invocation of the Holy Spirit).

Work on the Mass: the moment of the offering.

The first presentation of baptism.

Cammie (age three) meditates on the waters of Baptism at the Episcopal Church of the Angels, Pasadena, California.

Neal (age five) enters into the infancy narrative of the Annunciation at Good Shepherd Center, St. Paul, Minnesota.

Laura (age five) meditates on the Adoration of the Shepherd at Messiah Episcopal Church, St. Paul, Minnesota.

A celebration to solemnize the children's return from their first communion retreat: The children have carried in procession the small statue of the Good Shepherd, the candle and the box in which are placed the names of the new communicants.

The child-
ren listen to the
readings, which
they have chosen
in advance; the
names of the new
communicants
are hung on a
card and placed
on the altar.

A celebration of Pentecost: After the children have set out the seven candles and placed the names of the gifts of the Holy Spirit beneath them, the children then listen to the account and reading of the descent of the Holy Spirit.

Celebration of Pentecost: After the reading, Marco lights his candle from the candle that bears the name of the Spirit's gift he most wants.

Alain and friend contemplate Christ's gift of himself at the Last Supper.
South Bend, Indiana.

Pope John Paul II visits the atrium of Nostra Signora Di Lourdes Parish
in Rome.

A group of children celebrate the Last Supper. Good Shepherd
School, Cleveland, Ohio (U.S.A.).

A group of children reflect following the presentation of the parable
of the "merchant and the pearl." Toronto (Canada).